UBER EMPOWERMENT

By Nancy Hovde

Creative Dreams Publishing
Redondo Beach, CA

Published by Creative Dreams Publishing, Redondo Beach, California

Published simultaneously in Canada.

Published by:
Creative Dreams Publishing
P.O. Box 7000-642
Redondo Beach, CA 90277

For information please visit:
www.uberempowerment.com

Library of Congress Catalog-in-Publication Data
Hovde, Nancy.
Uber Empowerment/Nancy Hovde.-1st ed.
ISBN 978-0-9846057-0-5 (paperback)
1. Success 2. Spiritual Life 3. Personal Coaching. I. Title
2010908997
First paperback edition: July 2010

Cover photo used under license by iStockPhotos.com

Cover and Layout
Kelly Hewkin, Intuitive Graphic Design, www.intuitivegraphicdesign.com

Uber Defined:
A term with literal meaning of "above" in German.
The ultimate, above all, the best,
top, something that nothing is better than.

Acknowledgments

I am thankful for the Infinite Source that helped me to define, clarify and really listen to the guidance that wants to be communicated through out this book. Forever grateful to all of you who have inspired me to never give up in the pursuit of my dreams-you know who you are.

I am grateful for my sister, Priscilla, who has always believed in me and this book, her feedback, encouragement and enthusiasm that this book will put people on the path to success and authenticity in everything they are looking for.

I feel so blessed for all of the men and women who have supported me and encouraged me to write this book and share what I have learned, in order to pass it on to others and to make a difference in the World. Many of these men and women I am fortunate to have met through social media, such as Facebook and LinkedIn and your non-stop support and encouragement to bring this book of knowledge and wisdom into the world, inspired me to the end.

Thank you to my clients who have allowed me to coach and inspire them in knowing their secrets, issues and goals. It is from these experiences, that I have been guided to write and enlighten others throughout this book. In addition to those experiences, I am grateful for my authentic gifts and deeply grateful to my Higher Power for choosing me to bring this work to myself and others.

I am truly amazed with the special connection and joy of working with Kelly Hewkin, of Intuitive Graphic Design, on the formatting and book cover design. I could count on her professionalism, creativity and most of all, enjoying the whole process from start to finish, made working together fun and very meaningful.

*All the client examples through out this book were based on actual sessions. The client names have been changed to honor their confidentiality. It is with appreciation and gratitude that they are acknowledged in their anonymity for their contribution to this book.

Contents

Preface

"Embracing Life, Learning and Sharing Knowledge"
- Nancy Hovde

A book for guidance, motivation and inspiration and most of all, for growth in your life and reaching your Uber Self in Life. This book was designed to guide you to create your unique lifestyle plan that will empower you to feel your Best, discover your Authentic Self, and to feel empowered to BE your Uber Authentic Self.

Uber Empowerment was created from a deep place inside of me. This book has offered me a tremendous opportunity to share my knowledge, experiences and my inner journey. I feel I have an inner guide, inner strength and my faith and the knowledge that I have been intuitively drawn to, during my research for this book, and even long before I began this book, has allowed me to accept the messages and be in a willingness state of self, a true willingness and strong desire to want to share with others. An enlightened energy flows through me when I write and connects me to a greater creative awareness and consciousness, and this same greater creative awareness and consciousness, may arise in you, as you read and connect to this book.

Keep this book close and turn to it often. Take your time reading it. Know you can turn to this book as you need to. Once you have finished reading this book, for a dose of inspiration, take time to reflect on how you can use these guidelines for inspiration in wellness habits, mindset and lifestyle balance. And when you have a challenging situation, or you are being hyper-critical on yourself and/or others, when you feel frustrated, disappointed, turn to this book for re-directing you to your Uber Empowered Self. And when you are feeling your Uber Self, you can still enjoy re-reading the sections that most resonate with you and use it to apply and maintain the Ten Elements, along with my tools for lifestyle empowerment into your life, to stay inspired and share your new wisdom with others.

My Warmest Blessings to You,
Nancy Hovde
www.uberempowerment.com

Introduction

Discover your Uber Empowered Self and start living a life you will truly love. Is anything holding you back, if so what? Choose to embrace empowerment and I will provide you the tools and help inspire you, with each step, along your journey.

All of us can become Uber. Uber defined, is a term with literal meaning of "above" in German; the ultimate, above all, the best, top, something that nothing is better than. We can all reach our peak level in all areas of our lives. Your Uber Self involves the Whole Person you are – all the aspects that make up wonderful YOU: physical body, mind, emotions, soul/spirit.

Reaching your Uber level, is your own individual level, that you reach at your own pace. Perhaps you have experienced, like I have, physical injuries, low energy on different types of diets that were not right for you, not allowing enough time for "all those things you've always wanted to do, if you had the time" and not fully recognizing your greatest strengths and natural gifts that allow you to be your Uber best in life.

These experiences have led me to inspire my clients to realize, there is more to life and to live it fully and with passion. By applying Holistic Approaches to ensure they are feeling their best physically and mentally, living their true core values in life each day or as often as possible, and letting go of limited belief patterns, has allowed my clients to feel empowered to become their Uber Authentic Self in all areas of their life.

Finding it is one thing and then being able to maintain a balanced Uber Empowered Self is even more important. Realizing the need to be able to hang in there with the way your own individual energy will shift – we all have energy flow and energy that seems to ebb, at times. It is all in how we deal with the ebb and flow of our energy. Honoring times when we should slow down our pace in life, finding the balance between exercise and rest, the balance between work and play, love and alone time, and the balance between eating well most of the time and enjoying an indulgence now and then. Not expecting perfection from our selves all the time, but seeing positive progress. Being open to change and letting go of the past – to allow the newness and all that life has to show us – being able to stretch and be flexible physically as well as adjusting to life's changes.

This book explains a three tier process to achieve your Uber Empowered Self. I will guide you through each of the three tiers, every step, to recognize and become your Uber Authentic Self. The first Tier is designed to help you feel your best so you can think with your best clarity. In the Second Tier, you will learn and complete self-discovery exercises, that will help you recognize your Uber Self. Lastly, Tier Three will provide you with strategies to become your Uber Empowered Self, even when life throws you challenges.

As you read through this book and begin to use my tools as a guide into implementing your own Uber Empowerment Lifestyle Plan, my hope is, that you will find your own powerful inner spirit and that you gain flexibility and balance to live your life fully with passion in all areas of your life, while using knowledge to apply to anything daily life has in store for you.

TIER ONE
Feeling & Thinking Your Uber Best

To feel and think your Uber best requires that you begin to live a healthy lifestyle using your inner guidance and applying mindfulness to achieving your Uber Self. Living a healthy lifestyle begins like this:

- Choosing lifestyle choices using intuition, staying connected and applying specific mindset elements.

- Understand which nutrition plan will help you feel your Uber best and selecting foods mindfully for energy, inner and outer awareness.

- Develop your exercise plan that offers creative, empowering movement and energy for your mind, body and soul.

- Create effective lifestyle strategies for balance and stress management.

Making the most of our lives, everyday through healthy and positive lifestyle choices for our bodies-nourishing them physically, emotionally, mentally and spiritually. How wonderful life is when we take the best care of ourselves through healthy nutrition, enjoying a favorite form of exercise, managing stress and nourishing our souls, in order to share all of this knowledge with others.

Your results you are seeing in your life are because of your choices. One can choose their true path in life and develop the knowledge, experience and even the skill, but willingness, an action plan and accountability determines if one truly succeeds with their intentions, goals and dreams on their path. You deserve the best in life and to feel and become Uber Empowered.

When we choose to live a healthy lifestyle as our first priority, then our most effective creation and gifts to offer to others can happen. When we FEEL our Best, we can THINK our Best and BE our Best. This allows us to experience more energy, physically as well as to experience better clarity in our thinking, in order to discover our greatest strengths and natural gifts to offer others. We can then be empowered to be who we are and were meant to be.

Over the course of Tier One, I will step you through the process of creating the first part of your individual Uber Empowerment Lifestyle Plan, a structure that will support you in feeling your best, thinking your best and being your best.

"I believe in you, may this bring hope to your heart and wings to your dreams"
- Nancy Hovde

CHAPTER 1

Holistic Lifestyle Choices
Using Intuition & Staying Connected

A day dawns, quite like other days; in it, a single hour comes,
quite like other hours; but in that day and in that hour
the chance of a lifetime faces us.
- Maltbie Babcock

You are probably wondering what type of traits make up an Uber Empowered individual? I think there are many positive qualities that make up an Uber Empowered person. First, this individual is a health conscious achiever in life. They believe in taking the best care of their health and overall well-being. I am fully convinced that the additional individual traits and qualities, of an Uber Empowered person, would be having the right Mindset Approach, that consists of those qualities such as awareness, discipline, commitment, focus and most of all Ultimate Will, to become their Uber Self, can help to empower an individual and support a positive outlook on life. I truly believe taking the best care of yourself, along with the right Mindset Approach and living your authentic true core values in life, will carry you further on your path toward your Uber Empowered Self.

Keep in mind, that the Uber Self is Whole and One. I am going to show you how to maintain these characteristics and how to stay in alignment with your true, Uber Empowered Self. In life and science, many people like to isolate things and then study and research them in order to understand them, but every time we do that, we are missing out on the Whole, because everything is connected. We have now seen an incredibly fast moving shift in our thoughts on the body. A lot of us need to sit up and think about why looking at the body in such a segregated manner is really missing out on the Holistic Connection. The brain's neurotransmitters communicate disease or vibrant health to our body's organs and tissues based on our lifestyle choices we make each day. Through my research I have come to realize that in spirituality and science, we are one in the universe and we create our environment, we can't escape the reality that everything is always changing and nothing is really permanent, our energy and our vibrations create everything, and everything has a different vibration. So our thoughts had better be positive–as much as possible!

There are many ideas, tips, guidelines you can tailor to your own needs. I think the best plan laid, is when you can come up with your own lifestyle nutrition plan – that fits you, that you can be sane with and you can live with and feel it is your lifestyle and way of life and NOT "a diet". Along with finding your own nutrition plan, included in this would be developing your own balance in life and what works for you each day – how much time to spend on work, how much time to spend with your significant other, your family, how much time to spend on your training and running/working out. Lastly, included in this plan is discovering your true core values and ensuring you live these true core values every day or as often as possible. You can create, achieve and maintain your own Uber Empowerment Lifestyle Plan.

Much of what we need to do for our selves, in the way of nutrition, fitness/exercise, managing stress and in making life decisions, we already know. It can be very intuitive. We just need to listen! Intuition is your soul talking to you, that nudge you feel somewhere inside your body, the nagging thought in your head, the loving whisper of wisdom that is trying to get your attention to follow the right choice that is for your highest good and those around you.

To be connected, always – is the key to finding your energy that will empower you to perform your Uber Best & be balanced in all areas of your life. My hope is that this book will guide you to create your own Uber Empowerment Lifestyle Plan that will allow you to perform your personal best in all areas of your life and maintain a balanced Uber Empowerment Lifestyle. Life is precious. Life is fast. If we live fully in the present and try to do everything with mindfulness, we can enjoy a truly enriched life. We may as well feel our Uber best! We can find what our "Uber Best" feels like through nutrition, exercise, health and wellness and most of all with love in our lives. Love for life. Love for others. Love for yourself and of all things.

The reality is everything is connected – Mind, Body, and Soul. And our Spirituality – our Heart – which also is our cardiovascular system, makes each person Whole.

How do we begin to know what it feels like when we are truly connected to ourselves? What our needs are down to our core being is how. Knowing your needs – what do you need right now? Get use to asking yourself this, often. "Check in"… begin each day with enough time, a few minutes of alone time is ideal. Not rushing out the door. Visualize how you wish your day to unfold and know who you wish to connect with and how you want each encounter to go. If you have a race that day, visualize how well you will perform. Imagine how you want to feel for the day. If you have an important meeting with a potential account or client, visualize the professional connection becoming stronger and growing into a positive relationship. Then, ask yourself what is it you need to nourish your body to feel good, right now? Are you physically hungry for nourishing food? Is your body craving to move and stretch? Does your soul need spiritual nourishment?

Being in Tune With Your Uber Self Through Positive Thoughts

Is your interior in tip-top shape? I have come to notice, that older adults who develop a strong sense of spiritual self – whether through religion, meditation, or connecting with nature – need fewer hospitalizations and less long-term care than not-so-spiritual people. In all of my research, I am still not quite positive about what the connection is, but the stress-reducing nature of a strong belief system could make the all-important health difference.

For some people, spirituality is synonymous with religious activities; for others, it comes from different sources. Regardless, overall health seems to benefit when you're in tune with your inner self. Find activities that give meaning and purpose to your life, that help you become more aware of the world and your place in it, and that help you feel connected to others, yourself, or – if you choose – the divine. Your whole self – mind, body and soul – will be better for it.

Your conscious thoughts are crucial to your state of health. I believe our conscious thoughts create and re-create our physical body. I find it so fascinating, the study of the mind-body connection and how it is backed by science and can explain how emotions are associated with the physical changes in the body. Our perceptions, our outlook on life, how we interpret events and our experiences in our lives – change stress hormone levels of cortisol, epinephrine, and nor epinephrine. Chronic fear, hateful thoughts, resentment, sorrow, and depression raise stress hormone levels. When these levels remain elevated, insulin increases and cause the release of inflammatory hormones known as cytokines and leukotrienes. This leads to inflammation at the cellular level-the basis for cancer, arthritis, and all other diseases. Chronically elevated stress hormone levels are associated with metabolic syndrome, obesity, diabetes, osteoporosis, cancer, and cardiovascular disease.

I believe the law of attraction works very strongly in our lives. Whatever we think about the most, with the highest emotional intensity, is what we attract into our lives. Basically, our thoughts and beliefs lead to emotions. These emotions influence our behavior. These thoughts and emotions cause their physical equivalents to manifest in our lives and in our bodies. This happens because our consciousness communicates with our autonomic nervous system to carry out our beliefs and thoughts on a physical level. I am now careful of allowing myself to have thoughts of "I don't want catch that flu bug that is going around". And subconsciously, our mind doesn't have any signs for the words "don't" or "no". Our body hears: "Catch that flu bug-don't." The "catch flu bug" part becomes emphasized. These emphasized thought patterns, over time carries over to our physical body and over time we get what we think about and worry about the most. I try to think about leading an active, healthy life and then this is what's most likely to become a reality for me. Focusing on this wisdom is one of the most effective ways to change life for the better.

Positive affirmations and quotes are also nice to refer to. These affirmations and inspirational quotes can keep us uplifted and thinking positive thoughts. They can confirm to us, we are on our true path. Some of the most lovely moments in life are when we resonate with those "meant to read" words that seem to jump out at us while reading. It is nice to share these positive affirmations and inspirational quotes with others at times. Sometimes, you may have no idea that someone needed to hear one of the affirmations you just laid your eyes on, the quote may have reminded you of a pleasant memory or even brought to mind a friend you have not heard from in awhile or just someone out of the blue. Listen to your intuition and e-mail them or call them and tell them about the quote and how the quote made you think of them. Shared knowledge makes life richer. We will be exploring and discussing positive affirmations in more detail through out this book.

Ten Elements to Integrate With Daily Experiences

It is up to you, this is your life and it is your responsibility for achieving the outcomes you would like to see in your life-feeling more energetic and healthy, feeling more balanced between career and personal life, experiencing a better quality of life or maybe it is to finish a race. Together, we will create an Uber Empowerment Lifestyle Plan – this is a plan that requires a true dedication, applying the Ten Elements, the tools and guidelines I will be providing you with, along with practice and improvement each day.

Your Uber Empowerment Lifestyle Plan will include an individual healthy lifestyle plan, your Authentic True Core Values, goals, action and accountability steps. A will to thrive will emerge, once you have made a choice to commit to becoming your Uber Self and creating your Empowerment Plan. A positive attitude and self-care actions that drives you in the pursuit of personal fulfillment will give you the strength to by pass any obstacle or distractions and focus on your outcome, your results you want to see happen in your life. Listed below are The Ten Elements you will need to begin practicing, to develop the right mind set, if you are going to achieve your Uber Self. I would like you to keep these Ten Elements in mind through out your reading.

TEN ELEMNTS TO INTEGRATE WITH DAILY EXPERIENCES

AWARNESS

ACCEPTANCE

WILLINGNESS

DESIRE

DISCIPLINE/SELF LOVE

COMMITMENT

ARRANGE FOR SUCCESS

MONITOR YOUR ACTIONS/ACCOUNTABILITY

BALANCE

HAPPINESS

Will Lead To:

FEELING, THINKING & BEING
YOUR UBER SELF!

Awareness/Acceptance

First, we need to have *Awareness* in our life that is showing us or telling us or even nagging at us that we need a change. If the word change is actually holding you back from moving forward in your life, consider using Self Improvement. This Awareness can help us with *Acceptance* to the idea of change and Self Improvements. How do we fully Accept that we can make a change or a Self Improvement? We can accept the way things are, for right now; remembering that nothing is permanent. We do this through accepting our selves through Self Love by making Self Care and Self Nurturing positive healthy habits in our life. When we FEEL our Best, We tend to THINK our Best and we can then BE our best and provide our best gifts and strengths to others and live our life purpose. Being in optimal balance can also help turn thoughts that are confusing into clarity — when we FEEL our Best we tend to THINK our best and DO our best and so whatever choices we make, we have a better chance at moving forward with a positive attitude.

Willingness/Desire

Once we have become Aware of a change we want to make in our life and fully Accept that a change needs to be made, we can now go within and ask ourselves where are we right now, in our life — do we want to stay in the same old repetitive patterns we are so comfortable with but they are no longer showing much result or are we at a place in our life where we can become humble and be open and allow ourselves to evolve by learning something new that can help us see new results? If your answer is a true "yes" then you have arrived at a *Willingness* to grow. Willingness is to allow yourself to experience self-growth and personal development. True Willingness is all about you, that it is your idea to make a change, for yourself first. Willingness offers you a choice to make and for lasting results, it needs to be YOUR choice.

Willingness creates a strong *Desire* to become curious to life, to become more in tune with yourself and a Desire to develop a "knowing" that there is a higher level for you to live your life at. Desire offers seeking out, requesting for strength and courage to help you reach your goal.

Discipline/Commitment

Knowing you hold the Willingness and Desire within you, you now need to use *Discipline* to get there. Discipline is needed and is not always easy, especially when trying to let go of daily habits that don't serve your highest self such as too much sugar in your diet or not getting enough daily exercise, drinking too much, or working too much. Maybe you are just not allowing enough time for yourself? It can help to have a supportive friend to call or hire a personal trainer or a lifestyle coach that you will be accountable to. Often, it can help to have new, fresh perspective on Discipline and see Disciple as Self-Love. You are then able to be "disciplined" because you love yourself enough to see the results you would like to see in your life.

When you realize you can handle being more Disciplined then you certainly can *Commit* to whatever it takes to reach your goal and get to this higher level that you *just know* is waiting for you to discover. Commit to sticking with your lifestyle choices. Creating a personal agreement or vision statement can help motivate you to stay committed and be successful with your choices and goals in life. I will be walking your through, step by step, on creating your personal lifestyle statement, in Tier Two.

Arranging for Success/Monitor Your Actions

You've made the Commitment – congratulations! (Well, almost). Now, it is crucial that you come up with a solution, a plan on how you will get there. This means *Arranging for Success*. Coming up with your own Uber Lifestyle Empowerment Plan (relax because I'm going to guide you on how to come up with your very own!). Arranging for Success means creating a solution. What action steps can you take each day, big or small, that will keep you moving toward seeing more of what you want in your life and not away from what you want to see more of in your life?

Once your plan is created the next element called Arranging for Success is *Monitoring Your Actions*. Ah-ha! Yes, you will have to watch out for yourself and become much, much more in tune, with what you are doing right each day and what you are doing wrong each day, that is either assisting in moving you forward or is holding you back, from becoming your Uber Self. You will see results by monitoring your actions through accountability — you'll be quite surprised at what some of the small changes can make in your life and totally amazed at how even larger changes really can impact your quality of life.

Balance in Life/Happiness

Once you have Arranged for Success and have started to practice Monitoring your Actions, living a life in Balance is necessary for Happiness to be in your life. Living with inner awareness and appreciating how those simple things in life, like watching a sunset, can bring contentment and simplicity to life. Recognize that when you are in balance and harmony with all life's situations and those around you, you can trust that everything is the way it is meant to be. Reminding yourself

16

that where you are, today, right now on your journey, is just where you are meant to be. We will learn in more depth how to bring and maintain Balance and Happiness into our life, later in this book.

All of these tools, guidelines and resources I am going to provide you with, *will* require you to approach all of them with the mind set of the Ten Elements to achieve your Uber Self. I will provide you with guidelines and tools that will help you hold yourself accountable AND reach your goals. Keep reading!

Uber Self Improvements

You are probably aware of some improvements you would like to make in your life to feel and think your Uber best. In Tier One, you will explore how you can feel your Uber best and think your Uber best, through applying your intuition and knowledge, to create the following areas for Tier One on your Uber Empowerment Lifestyle Plan: nutrition planning, creative and energetic movement and managing stress that will allow you to live a balanced lifestyle.

I would like you to think about what you could improve upon in your life to feel and think your Uber best. What improvements could you make in your nutrition choices? Or perhaps you are already aware of which foods make you feel your Uber best and think your Uber best but you would like to make improvements in physical activity or developing new therapeutic remedies for stress management? Which of these areas in your life would you like to change or improve in? Will there be major improvements you would like to make or some minor improvements? Or maybe there are some areas you would just like to fine tune a bit.

Take some time to reflect on the improvements you would like to make for nutrition, exercise/physical activity and managing stress in your life. Write these on your Uber Empowerment Lifestyle Plan.

You now are aware of the Uber Self Improvements you want to work on. Accept the current place you are in your life right now and what is currently keeping you from staying in the same situation and the same patterns. I'd like you to add these thoughts to your list of your Self Improvements. You may find you want to just start with one improvement for now. Once you've made this list, read it over again. Go deep with in and ask yourself the following questions:

> *First, ask yourself how willing am I to make this change (or these changes)? Create a want with in yourself. Have you arrived at a place in your life where you are absolutely fed up with the same old results you see no matter what you've tried? Is this change you want to make really something you yourself WANT to do or have you been attempting to make this change for someone else? A true want is putting you in a state of willingness. This is good.*

> *Next, create a WHY with in yourself. What is the true reason you want to change? This will create a true desire in you and will often be a motivational reason to refer to again and again to help keep you on track and to ultimately reach your goal.*

Let's look at this example. When Cassandra came to me for my lifestyle coaching services, she had always been active and loved to run and enjoyed her career. When she got married, to her husband, Brian, her exercising routine began to change. While they had dated this was not an issue, since they were not always together and each lived in their own

18

home, Cassandra was able to fit in work/career and her workouts on a consistent basis.

Cassandra didn't give it much thought, until now. Being married and together every day, slowly, this began to change Cassandra's lifestyle habit of consistent workouts. She soon began to lack energy and didn't seem to have that unique edge about her and mental sharpness and even her sense of humor seemed to dwindle and most of all her patience – with her husband, her co-workers and friends. At first, she was not aware why this happened. She loved her husband and since they were both such busy career minded people, she loved spending each opportunity they had together.

It took a true friend who finally pointed this out to Cassandra. My client was now *aware* and this made sense. Cassandra *accepted* this as true. And she wanted to make an improvement with her attitude and was *willing* to do whatever it took to make time for her running again, so her attitude would once again become more positive, as well as for positive physical health reasons. She *desired* to achieve a healthy and positive attitude through a consistent workout schedule. Cassandra added this to her Self Improvement list. She desired to enjoy a richer life, a better quality of life – for her health, her marriage, her relationships in life with her friends and co-workers and most of all for herself and feeling happy with her attitude on life.

The desire is there – great. Now, we need to make this happen! In order for an Uber Self Improvement to become reality, we need to implement the next elements of *Arranging for Success* and *Monitoring Our Actions/ Accountability*. In Cassandra's case, she was willing to arise an hour early on the mornings she wanted to run. And since she also considered herself a flexible runner – meaning that she was not either a morning runner or an afternoon runner, she chose to make her running schedule flexible with alternating mornings and afternoons. This worked well with both my client and her husband's career schedule. The way Cassandra *monitored her actions* was with *commitment* and *discipline/self-love*, every day. She kept a journal log of her workouts and the progress she made. The results she began to see in her Self Improvements motivated her to stick with her Uber Self Empowerment Plan and she soon felt much more *balance* and *happiness* in her life. She felt like her Uber Self.

By creating your Uber Empowerment Lifestyle Plan and staying committed, disciplined and monitoring your actions through accountability, will help you reach your goals. You will find commitment and discipline are achievable when your mind is focused and in the moment through out the day, remembering to stay aware of what your needs are, accepting where you are, right now and how you are feeling. Taking time for reflection through out the day and always making time for a self-care act, that might include therapeutic remedies for the mind, exercise and healthy foods for the body and nourishment for the soul. Self-Care acts communicate Self-Love.

Remember the Self Improvements you want to create – read your list of the Self Improvements again and re-connect with the feeling of willingness and desire. Once you have connected again with that emotional response that is leading you to a strong pull – a yes I want to see Uber Self Improvements in my life, stay on track by staying committed and disciplined to your Uber Lifestyle Empowerment Plan. Your heart has a way of guiding you in choosing what is right for YOU. Something inspiring that seems to happen when listening to the spirit and love within. If all your energies & focus are going in the same direction, life just seems to flow a little better and amazing things can happen.

We have just explored how you can empower yourself by learning to trust your intuition when choosing the right lifestyle choices for *you* and integrating the Ten Mindset Elements to achieve your goals, make self improvements and to use in your daily experiences.

In the next chapter, you will begin creating Tier One of your Uber Empowerment Lifestyle Plan. You will discover how the choices you make in the foods you select each day, can have a positive or a negative effect on your overall well-being and either help you or keep you from enjoying a quality lifestyle, and in some cases, from reaching your desired goals and intentions in life. This is the first and most important choice you can empower yourself with – it all starts here. Mastering this area in your life will bring you much closer, much faster, to feeling and thinking your Uber Best so you can be your Uber Self in life.

I would like to make a note, if you honestly feel you are already eating the best diet for yourself, that allows you to feel and think your best, and you find that your exercise schedule allows you to feel energized and connected at the mind, body and soul levels; you know you are living a balanced life and managing stress, then feel free to move onto Tier Two. But, I encourage you to read chapters two, three and four because you may find a method or knowledge you would like to integrate into your lifestyle.

CHAPTER 2

Nutrition: Choosing Foods
With Mindfullness & Intuition For Energy,
Inner & Outer Awarness

"To eat is a necessity, but to eat intelligently is an art."
- La Rochefoucauld

Would you like to become more aware of how self-love and self-care for the mind, body and soul can help you choose healthy habits such as the right foods for your body that will have a positive effect on your over all well-being and help you to feel your optimal in life? Would you like to develop a true appreciation for thinking more about the effectiveness of your exercise routine and what's going on inside the body? Too many people, year after year, get stuck doing the same workout routine, with very little thought, as to what's happening within the body. Sometimes, this can lead to inflexiblity, both physically and mentally, living by the same ineffecitve patterns in daily life, year after year.

I know for me, 90% of my health and wellness, is the nutritional foods I am putting into my mouth. I've seen many frustrated individuals who workout for hours at the gym and are hoping for a certain look they want or hoping to get to a certain level of fitness and what many of them don't realize, sadly, is that so much of what they see in the mirror and are currently unhappy with, is exactly what they have been putting into their mouth. They don't realize how important *what* they eat is. They get caught up in a vicious cycle of exercising to "burn off" the food they ate the night before. Never making changes or tweaks in their diet. This will not get you to feeling and thinking your Uber best.

Perhaps you are already eating a healthy diet and you just want a bit of fine tuning to get to the level that allows you to perform at your best. Youmay not have found which type of foods will help to pull you through your day for optimal energy and clarity. You may be wondering why certain foods make you feel more fatigued or congested. Figuring out which foods may be causing you to feel sluggish, will make a huge difference in your energy level and how you think and perform. This takes mindfulness, patience and some effort on your part, such as expanding your awareness and knowledge, through reading this book and most of all, learning to trust what your body is intuitively trying to tell you.

I used to train, day after day, totally caught up in the number of miles I was logging and number or workouts I could squeeze in, instead of stepping back and learning what could make me feel more energetic and reach my Uber Self level, with less time spent at the gym and more time living a balanced life.

My hope is that all of my research on the various diets, as well as finding the key nutrients and supplements to include in your nutrition plan, will help you with making positive lifestyle choices and that all of this knowledge will present a fresh and emotionally healthy way to look at eating.

Developing a healthy way to look at eating, is important information that needs to be discussed. Since I've been a "picky eater" for years and have heard all of the possible responses to eating the way I do, now these comments about my diet, are being backed with so much research and science, showing just how important a clean, organic and nutritious diet is, that I have become a very Proud Picky Eater. What is a "picky eater"? Ever since I can remember, my family termed me a "picky eater". A quote written in my Baby Book from my mom: "your eating habits are not the best but are improving. You like chocolate foods very much". Okay, well, that has not changed, in the fact, I do enjoy the occasional piece of dark chocolate. However, things did improve and very well, too. Probably, better than my mom had anticipated – I now actually love vegetables. Included in a clean, organic and nutritious diet, is really knowing which foods make *you* feel *your* best, allowing you to become a Proud Picky Eater. Just because a diet may include organic foods, this does not always indicate that all organic foods are good for *you*. You will discover which foods allow you to feel and think your best.

It is important to know, that sometimes it can be quite a challenge when you make a final lifestyle choice to commit to a nutrition and exercise plan that is right for you. Remember, that even daily small steps can help to make a big difference and keep love as your source of power, to acheive those Self Improvements you wish to create in your life. The encouraging news is that once you have mastered feeling and thinking your Uber best and have created Tier One on your Uber Empowerment Lifestyle Plan, the results are quickly noticeable, in how you feel and think and will inspire you to commit to your new Uber Empowered Lifestyle. This will motivate you to grow into tier two and tier three on your Uber Empowerment Lifestyle Plan.

Since you have picked up this book and have read this far, I am guessing you have a strong desire or some interest to improve your self in health, fitness or live a balanced and fully enriched life, at the Uber level. I am also guessing you have a strong desire to fine tune some of your eating habits and maybe even a strong desire for inner peace or looking for opportunities to use your natural gifts in life. Perhaps you would like to limit stress in your life. Good, because my knowledge I wish to share with you, has such goals in mind. In spending time reading this information contained within, it won't take long to see that my philosophy on success and happiness is: "we must FEEL our Best to THINK our Best; this allows us to BE our Best, so we can DO our Best – and offer our greatest gifts and strengths to the World and live our life purpose".

In Tier One, we will discuss practicing mind to movement in your workouts and mindfulness in your day to day life and most importantly, eating like the "picky person" that you are. I'm going to help you every step of the way, with your armor against what we've been told is "the normal way to eat", the pace at which we've been forced at times to adapt to in our life, that can cause us to make unhealthy choices – I will provide you with guidelines to shield yourself from those type of distractions. You will learn that it only feels normal when you choose positive and healthy lifestyle choices – through self love and self care rituals, nutrition and diet, creative movement and by staying balanced and deeply connected to your inner beliefs.

Some of you may need a bigger boost. So if you are feeling lack of motivation, read on. I will give you tips on how to overcome this feeling. Healthy food might seem boring and bland to you, right now. Plus, it takes ultimate will to eat healthfully. However, eating healthy foods can be exciting and tasty if you put forth some effort and apply the Ten Elements, integrated with your intution, toward eating, for nourishment, on all levels: mind, body and soul.

Take a few minutes to write down all the reasons you want to eat healthy. These reasons can be on your Uber Self Improvement List. For instance,

"I've been diagnosed with heart disease/insulin resistance/overweight/ chronic fatigue and need to start eating better, might be a few examples. I just feel better about myself when I eat properly, could be another reason. Another reason could be, "I have amazing energy when I exercise or play with my children, when I focus on healthy food choices and how these foods make me feel." Try to come up with as many reasons as possible. This will keep you strong and focused. Any time you have doubts and need motivation, you can think about your list. That's why you need to make sure it is meaningful.

Research shows a healthy diet can help ward off the blues. Diets that are abundant in produce, deliver lots of folate, which enhances communication in brain cells. Fruits and vegetables are also packed with anti-oxidants, which are linked to lower rates of depression. Research shows the long-chain Omega-3 fats, found in fish, may defend against depression by reducing inflammation in the brain. When we choose to follow a healthy lifestyle, we can feel our best, physically which will allow us to think with clarity and be our Uber Self.

As you are aware, there are many diets on the market all claiming to be The One that will help you feel your best. You can choose what to take away from the following information and suggestions to improve your day to day nutrition selections. The nutritional information I share with you is about lifestyle improvement ideas and tips to help you create your own system, not a diet. Although many of my clients have lost weight, this is not about weight-loss but creating your own nutrition plan that will help you feel and think your Uber best. My goal is to help you:

- Realize *why* there are so many benefits when you choose to take the best care of yourself through nutrition, exercise and managing stress by listening to your intuition and what your body is trying to tell you.

- Discover *how* to enjoy eating healthy and inspire you that you will feel your best when you are taking the best care of yourself.

- How empowered you can feel when you trust your intuition to guide you on what to eat, when to eat and how much to eat.

There is no one diet for everyone. We are all made up differently. Yet, we can all benefit with several key components that can be integrated into any nutrition plan:

- Developing Healthy Eating Patterns
- Choosing the right Nutritional Supplements
- Nourishing our Souls

Developing Healthy Eating Patterns

Athletes know they need to fuel their body to perform well. Educated and aware adults know they need to nourish their bodies with the right foods and supplements to feel energized and to increase their overall well-being. We all have stress in our lives and it is all in how we not only learn to, but commit to managing the stress. When we don't manage the stress in our lives, this can lead to overeating or not eating at all for many people. Have you thought about Physical vs. Emotional eating?

Overeating is actually caused by 75% from emotions. What leads to this emotional binge? For some of my clients, it can be an inability to focus and so they reach for caffeine and sugar. I encourage you to tell your doctor if you feel you have an emotional related overeating issue.

Other triggers that lead to emotional overeating are increased stress, life keeps getting busier, accessibility of food as a means to block feeling and not dealing with feelings at the time they surface, and physiological needs and some will get so busy they forget to eat. We need to express feelings. When a person gets so busy that they forget to eat, this can lead to cravings and then overeating is likely or choosing something unhealthy to eat.

It is important to make time to eat. And what if you are not living your core values every day or as often as possible? Did you ever think that this could be a type of frustration or stress that leads you reaching for one too many cocktails in the evening when what you really want and need, is to share a quality conversation with a close friend?

Some Potential Indicators of Emotional Eating are:

- it is a very sudden need
  (from urgent thoughts, stress) to eat;

- no physical signs (no stomach rumbling);

- and automatic or absent minded eating
  (hand to mouth).

- Guilt. People can get caught up in a vicious cycle
  – they may be feeling guilt and so they eat to cover up
  the guilt and then this leads to more guilt and so they
  eat more to keep covering up the feeling of guilt.

When a person experiences physical, healthy, normal signs of hunger, it can be seen as, it builds slowly and more gradual and is open to a variety of foods – usually something healthy and not a craving. It is based in the stomach and is focused on eating awareness and deliberate, healthy choices. This person will stop when full.

Stress is a huge cause for many people to overeat. In fact, high stress levels can lead to high cortisol levels. An example might be looking at women with either bulimia nervosa or anorexia nervosa – both with these issues might have stress in their lives that lead to their emotional eating. It is very important to manage stress, if we don't and our cortisol levels are high, this can lead to weight gain. High cortisol promotes protein to blood glucose which leads to weight gain.

How can we manage overeating? By being aware of our inner needs and ask ourselves a series of why questions. For example: I'm craving an extra cup of coffee this afternoon (let's say I have already had my usual morning 2 cups of coffee). Why am I craving an extra cup in the afternoon? I'm cold and it is raining outside. Hmm...... is this an emotional trigger? I think so. Does the fact that, it is raining outside and my thoughts of a steamy cup of coffee have to do with any childhood memories of being cared for or does this maybe trigger a different emotional memory? Keep asking "why". Get to the root of the trigger. A cup of green tea or steamy herbal tea would be a healthier choice.

Looking at patterns of eating is also a way to determine if you are overeating for emotional reasons. Develop an alternative solution. Ask yourself what else can you do to satisfy that need?

I have found the 15-minute Wait it Out & Self Check process to be a very effective method for not just overeating/reaching for something unhealthy to eat, but also for any type of unhealthy lifestyle choice or addiction/habit (smoking, drinking, gossiping, any negative type of behavior). "Check-In" with yourself at that moment. What is it you need right now? This can be a very good time to write, or what many refer to as Emotional Journaling. Write down your thoughts you are having at the moment, your feelings and refresh yourself with your list of reasons for prioritizing your health. You may find you need more or less time for your own Wait it Out & Self Check process and this is okay. A healthy lifestyle takes listening to your intuition, mindfulness, discipline and commitment just to name a few necessary components.

A physical release my also assist you in moving toward a healthy lifestyle choice instead of going for that unhealthy habit, addiction or negative lifestyle choice. A brisk walk – even 10 minutes and get some fresh air, deep breathing, or stretching exercises that allow you to go within and notice where you are holding any tension in your body.

I have several methods I have shared with clients to help them overcome unhealthy nutritional choices. When lack of time has been their excuse, providing my clients with the following suggestions in how to plan better has been an effective strategy:

1. For Americans rushing to get a healthy meal on the table between work, soccer, ballet class and sleep, time is often the missing ingredient. This lack of time leads many people to rely on unhealthy versions of takeout, fast food and easy-to-fix convenience foods.

   The truth is that it's not easy to eat healthfully when you're busy, particularly when it's not a priority in your life. Even if you have no time to buy healthy food and cook at home, you still have options. Let's do some planning.

2. You can make convenience and fast foods work for you. For instance, you can find out what healthy offerings you might enjoy at your favorite restaurant (try getting menus in advance). You can also try batch

cooking: picking one day of the week to prepare an entire week's worth of healthy meals.

3. A client of mine, Beth, found her favorite way to plan to eat healthy all week, is to use her creativity on weekends from buying to preparing food for the week. She likes to focus on color when buying fruits and vegetables. Usually, sometime on Sunday afternoon or evening, Beth would cook up some organic turkey breasts or chicken breasts-enough for a few days to a week. Beth would use these turkey and chicken breasts in salads, soups or have a side of green vegetables with them. You can get creative! Choose sauces that are lower in saturated or use just herbs. Get creative and try different ones. Just remember if you do use a sauce, there can be sugar in these (wrong kind of carbohydrates and also added sodium). Use sauces sparingly like for special occasions. I want to help you get to a healthier level. And surf the internet for research on some low fat, healthy sauces. If you must have sauces more often, keep the sauce on the side and dip your meat or vegetables. Access recipes and ideas on the internet to get more creative with making your sauces with less sodium and less sugar. I refer to the internet often, because it is up to date and always some new recipe to check out and keep your cooking world more interesting!

4. No matter how busy – DO NOT SKIP MEALS! Skipping meals leads to increased production of hormones that cause muscle loss. How silly would that be, to lose what you worked so hard in the gym to gain?! So, eat frequently 3 to 4 small meals and 2 to 3 snacks daily. (We will go more into detail on this later).

The more active individual may need between 4 and 6 small meals a day and 2 to 3 snacks, depending on your intensity of training.

5. Think to eat healthy is expensive? Hmm… well, that is not a good enough excuse either, in choosing to not eat healthy. Through my research I found in comparing unhealthy foods with healthy ones, it may seem cheaper and simpler to eat unhealthy foods. And in many cases it is. However, according to the USDA Economic Research Service Analysis, more than half of the 69 forms of fruit and 85 forms of vegetables included in the analysis were estimated to cost 25 cents or less per serving, and 86 percent of all vegetables and 78 percent of all fruits cost less than 50 cents a serving.

6. Plan your meals and shopping lists in advance. Search out coupons and specials on supermarket Web sites. To cut shopping time and avoid impulse purchases, write the list according to the grocery aisles and sections in the store. You probably know the store you shop in pretty well, but if you map it out, you will be more likely to stick to the plan. Bring your lunch to work or school. Don't wait until you're starving to eat. Also, keep in mind that unhealthy foods are often more expensive than healthier choices. For instance, one apple pie generally costs three times more than five apples.

7. What about the Unhealthy Food at Work excuse some of you may have? Yes, all the birthdays, celebration parties, co-workers bringing unhealthy foods and the stress of the workplace, the office can be a huge challenge for anyone trying to stay healthy.

- It is important to be social. Team up with a co-worker who is also determined to lose weight. An office diet buddy can provide you with emotional support and reminders.

- It takes some planning. Gather menus from all local restaurants as well as convenient takeout and fast-food eateries. Then scan them for healthy foods. Narrow your choices and highlight.

- Pack a healthy lunch: Bring your own slices of freshly cooked turkey. Perhaps you have some left over from the night before, or cook up enough to last you a few days. You can also do this with chicken and then put the turkey or chicken in salads or cut veggies.

- Many offices are breeding grounds for nibbling just because snack foods are available. Decide in advance what you will and will not eat.

  These are mostly filled with unhealthy choices. Bring your own healthy snacks. Raw nuts, low-carb/low sugar (but high quality) protein bars, fresh organic, chopped or cut veggies and fruit slices.

8. There Are Too Many Tempting Foods. This is by far the most common complaint and excuse for why we can't seem to eat healthfully. Everywhere you go there's fast food, cupcakes, doughnuts and fried chicken — the list is endless. In fact, many public health advocates call this an obese-friendly environment. So, yes, it's tough when you're trying to lose weight to eat healthfully. Planning is one of the only ways to

overcome the problem. Don't think simple willpower is going to get you past indulging in all those tempting foods. Plan ahead. Think about where you're going and what healthy foods will be available. Try to mentally rehearse making healthier choices in the most tempting situations. For instance, find the healthier choices on fast-food menus before you get there (most fast-food restaurants have information on their Web sites). When traveling or in stressful situations, keep healthy food (including ready-to-eat foods such as protein powders, low glycemic index protein bars, pre-cut organic vegetables and fruit, raw nuts) readily available.

9. Eating out frequently and traveling can also be a big challenge when trying to stick with your healthy lifestyle choices. In fact, up to 50 percent of our food budget is spent eating out, and foods purchased outside the home are generally higher in calories and saturated fat and lower in fiber and nutrients than home-prepared foods. There is a solution though that has helped me and also some of my clients who've shared their suggestions.

There are lots of ways to eat out and still eat healthfully. Start by picking places that offer healthy choices. Also, follow a few of these tips:

- Limit mayo, tartar sauce, creamy dressings and extra cheese.

- Ask for dressing, sauces, butter or sour cream on the side. I suggest using Olive Oil for your salad dressing, is has plenty of mono-saturated fat and poly-saturated fats; drizzle this on steamed veggies and salads.

- Use mustard, ketchup, salt, pepper or vinegar as fat-free ways to season your food.

- Watch nuts, croutons and other salad add on items. (Portion size important!).

- Chicken and fish are good choices only if they're grilled or broiled, NOT breaded or deep-fried.

- Avoid large portions. Split your entrée with a family member, or ask for a half-portion.

- Read the menu. Avoid any of the following words: a la mode, au gratin (covered with cheese), battered, bisque, breaded, buttered, cheese sauce, creamy or rich, crispy, deep-fried, deluxe, fried, hollandaise (sauce made with butter and egg yolks), jumbo, scalloped, sautéed (unless you make a special request for it to be prepared in a small amount of oil) and tempura.

- Don't be afraid to ask questions or make special requests. (I do all the time. Just ask very politely-that is always appreciated).

- Ideally, if you can, choose a Trader Joe's or a Whole Foods when on the road for work or during your travels. Select something that has been prepared fresh in the deli section such as a garden salad, slices of turkey or chicken, fresh fruit. Both places have some smart and healthy choices, if you look for them. Whole Foods has a salad bar where you can mix your own salad along with other cooked items. They post the ingredients next to each dish, too. These two choices, Trader Joe's and Whole Foods is much better than a fast food joint.

These tips will help you to feel your inner power and remind you what your true self desires and how your true energy feels when you consistently make healthy lifestyle choices—all to keep you on your true path of feeling your Uber self.

On occasion, my clients will tell me they get certain overwhelming remarks and comments from some peers and family about their new eating habits. I realize that some of you may have family and friends who do not support your healthy nutritional choices. Certain friends and family members can really put a damper on your diet. Also, family can influence your behavior; if your spouse doesn't eat healthfully, it can make it difficult for you to eat right.

Don't let your family throw you off track. Set boundaries for yourself when dining out or eating at home, and make sure that you keep track of your difficult family eating situations and think in advance about how you're going to overcome them. Give yourself permission to eat different foods from the ones they're eating and remain on track. Also, remember to talk with your family and let them know you want their help – tell them not to police your eating, but to support your healthy eating choices.

I love to eat — but loving to eat, with mindfulness and eating with haste and thoughtlessness are two entirely different things. I think it is very important to regain a healthy perspective on food, if you do not already have a healthy relationship with food. I enjoy food – but what is more, I enjoy great food and eating with mindfulness. For example, I encourage you, next time you are eating a meal, focus on how you are digesting your food. Become more aware of what you are eating by paying attention to your senses. What kind of herbs do you taste? Can you name all of them? What other flavors and aromas are you taking in? Did you choose enough color for this meal? (Remember, the more colors in your food, the more phyto-nutrients you are getting in your diet). Give gratitude for each meal, as this increases awareness as well. And remember to sit and reflect after you finished your meal. This can help with both digestion and assimilation.

I find eating is a pleasant experience and I hope you will, too. Preparing a meal is not just some random food thrown together and then heated up on the stove or cooked until it is warm; it is an activity of both creative thought and commitment. It involves awareness and mindfulness just like everything else in life. Eating will begin to take on a whole new meaning to you when it means the difference between feeling healthy and having clarity in your life instead of just staying in the same routine and feeling stuck in a rut. Eating right can motivate you, energize you, support positive thoughts and you can feel happy instead of sluggish and feeling like a looser. Food is your friend and nourishes you to feel your best and think your best and become your Uber best.

You can continue to enjoy the occasional holiday and birthday dinner celebration, etc. Moderation and balance would be the key, of course. And notice I said "occasional".

This information I provide to you, as well as additional information you should research on your own, will help you to know which foods can support you to feel your Uber Best Self. And remember, you really do not need to justify why you eat the foods you do to others. I would like to share one of my favorite quotes by Mark Twain with you:

"Keep away from people who try to belittle your ambitions. Small people always do that, but the really great make you feel that you, too, can become great."

It is always a choice – your choice in eating healthy and having a healthy relationship with food. It can feel like a source of embarrassment or a source of empowerment. So take pride in the fact that your kitchen cabinets have little-or-no saturated fat, stay connected to your inner beliefs and hold your head up high as you make a special request when ordering out and celebrate your choice to be a Proud and Picky eater. Besides, a huge benefit of eating a diverse diet that is low in saturated fat calories and high in nutrients can make you feel and look younger.

Nutrition vs. Diet & Which Nutrition Plan Will Help You Feel Your Uber Best?

In my research and own personal experience with nutrition and optimal wellness, I have found the greatest success when the goal is to feel my best and think my best. Choosing to focus on nutrition versus diet by focusing on nutrition and the biochemical processes that result from the foods and beverages we ingest. Our bodies utilize the food substances for growth, repair, and maintenance of activities in the body, as a Whole. How your body absorbs, digests, metabolizes and assimilates these food substances is very individual. Foods we eat have a huge role on digestion, gastrointestinal health, neurotransmitter response, immune function, metabolic shifts and reactions and pathways of detoxification.

Remember, it is always best to approach your diet according to what is best for you not necessarily what is standard recommendation for those people who are confronted with a certain health related issue. This is why it is important to read the most recent nutrition research and know your unique biochemical make up. If you want to achieve your Uber best and feel you need exceptional professional guidance, beyond what my tools will provide you with, I suggest visiting a CCN – Certified Clinical Nutritionist or an M.D. who specializes in optimal wellness and anti-aging.

Preventative & Alternative Healthcare professionals realize that all individuals have unique metabolic patterns that affect their health needs – "one size does not fit all". So maybe some patients would benefit on a lifestyle program that is more directly related to their blood type or Metabolic Type, while others benefit more with a different therapeutic approach.

Here are just a few of the millions and millions of diet programs out there:

- The Raw Foods Diet
- The Zone Diet
- The South Beach Diet
- Low Glycemic Index Diet
- Blood Type Diet
- Metabolic Type Diet

In my personal experience and research, I discovered my individual nutrition plan that allows me to feel in optimal balance. The nutrition plan that allows me to feel my best and think my best. My theory is, I selected only the areas of the three different diets that most benefit me and focused only on those areas. You can do the same. I am going to briefly discuss the three diet programs that I found most benefit me. You can choose the same three or choose only one and blend with other diet plans. It is what works for you and the answers lay within you, you just need to listen and experiment.

1. Low Glycemic Index Diet

We can begin to feel our best and reach our Uber Self in our lives by nourishing our body with several small, balanced meals and by keeping our blood sugar level and our energy humming. This can be achieved by eating lean protein at every meal and the right type of fat and effective carbohydrates through out the day. When we take a look at a Low-Glycemic Index Diet, if you try this for one week, you'll find that cravings do go away. If you are training for something such as an upcoming race or if a woman is pregnant, you can be satisfied on a Low Glycemic Index diet – provided you include enough lean protein and the right carbohydrates and good fat and be aware of how much (portion size) your body will need during this time period.

It is important to choose the right type of carbohydrates. This can be done using the Glycemic Index (GI), which refers to the impact a food has on blood sugar response. Low GI foods tend to stabilize the blood sugar over a longer period of time, whereas higher GI foods cause a quick rise in blood sugar followed by a fast drop in blood sugar. This can lead to hypoglycemia in individuals who are sensitive to blood sugar swings.

Your energy levels will be much lower if you feast on foods with a high glycemic index such as doughnuts and cookies as opposed to whole grains, fruits, and vegetables, which have a much lower glycemic index. Keep in mind that not everyone will be sensitive to the glycemic index of foods. It is also important to note that multiple factors can affect the GI of a specific food, such as meal size, combinations of foods, and food preparation. Organic foods are preferable. Additional information can be found at www.glycemicindex.com.

The following is an example of Low, Medium and High Glycemic Index Foods.

Glycemic Index of Foods

Low (55 or less)	Medium (56-69)	High
Skim milk	Banana	Watermelon
Plain yogurt	Pineapple	Dried dates
Soy beverage	Raisins	Baked white potato
Apple/plum/orange	Brown rice	Instant rice
Sweet potato	Couscous	Bagel, white
Converted Rice	Basmati rice	Table sugar
Al dente pasta	Whole wheat bread	
Lentils/kidney/baked beans	Rye bread	

2. Metabolic Type

Depending on your Metabolic Type, some people feel much better on a higher carbohydrate, lower protein and fat diet. Other people feel better on a higher protein and fats and lower carb diet. We all have a different make-up. For an accurate diagnosis, a trained health practitioner can provide a thorough assessment that may include urine and blood tests.

Here is a bit of history behind Metabolic Type Diet. It goes back to the 1930's, dentist Weston Price, began expeditions around the world and uncovered the link between modern eating habits and chronic degenerative diseases. He also discovered that there was no one diet that would be healthy for all people — there was too much variation in climate, local produce, environmental conditions, heredity, genetics, culture.

In later years, George Watson, Roger Williams, William Kelley, and others continued research in this area. They believed that people's metabolisms functioned differently when it came to two factors, which are largely determined by heredity:

Autonomic nervous system dominance. There are two branches of this system. One of these branches, the sympathetic nervous system, is often referred to as the "fight or flight" branch. It helps you burn energy. The other branch is the parasympathetic nervous system. This branch helps you conserve energy. It also helps you digest food. Advocates of this diet believe that one branch tends to be stronger or more dominant than the other.

Rate of cellular oxidation. This refers to the rate at which cells convert food into energy. Some people are fast oxidizers, because they rapidly convert food into energy. In order to balance their systems, fast oxidizers need to eat heavier proteins and fats to that burn slowly. In contrast, slow oxidizers convert food into energy at a slow rate. In order to balance their systems, it's recommended that they eat mainly carbohydrates rather than protein and fat.

The guide lines for this type of diet would be:

Protein types should eat diets that are rich in protein, fats and oils, and high-purine proteins such as organ meats, pate, beef liver, chicken liver, and beef. Carbohydrate intake should be low.

Carbohydrate types should eat diets that are high in carbohydrates and low in protein, fats, and oils. They should eat light, low-purine proteins.

Mixed types should eat a mixture of high-fat, high-purine proteins and low-fat, low-purine proteins such as cheese, eggs, yogurt, tofu, nuts. This type requires relatively equal ratios of proteins, fats, and carbohydrates.

3. Blood Type Diet

I have also experimented with a diet that focuses on eating in relation to my blood type. Dr. Peter J. D'Adamo has written several books that relate to eating in relation to your blood type. Through my own extensive research, and experimenting on different types of diets, I have found that when I use this as just a guideline for myself, it seems to work well for me on which of the foods to avoid. Many of my clients have found when they focus on avoiding the suggested foods, they have more energy and seem to digest foods more effectively. In his book he suggests the following based on your blood type:

Blood Type O: High Protein/Low Carb: Eat meat (high protein, low carbohydrate) Original cavemen/women

- Beneficial foods: Sea food, meat, vegetables, fruit

- Foods to avoid: Grains, wheat, corn, brussel sprouts, cauliflower, kidney beans, navy beans, lentils, cabbage

Blood Type A: Tend to do well on a vegetarian diet (high carbohydrate, low fat) very much the opposite of Blood Type O.

- Beneficial foods: Vegetables, tofu, soy, seafood, grains, beans, legumes, fruit

- Foods to avoid: Meat, dairy, kidney beans, lima beans, wheat

Blood Type B: A varied and balanced diet of all the blood types, one including meat. This blood type seems to be one that does very well on dairy products, unlike Blood Types A and O and AB.

- Beneficial foods: Meat (no chicken), dairy, grains, legumes, vegetables, fruits

- Foods to avoid: Corn, lentil, peanuts, sesame, seeds, buckwheat, wheat

Blood type AB: Mixed diet in moderation. Tend to have the most benefits and intolerance of types A and B.

- Beneficial foods: Meat, seafood, dairy, tofu, beans, legumes, grains, vegetables, fruits

- Foods to avoid: Red meat, kidney beans, lima beans, seeds, corn, buckwheat, chicken

According to blood type, Dr. Peter J. D'Amamo explains we all have beneficial foods that can have a medicine effect on us and makes us feel good, neutral foods that act just as that, foods, to our bodies and that there are certain foods to avoid, so we can feel our optimal.

In my personal experience with this diet the benefits I found, were by avoiding the foods suggested to avoid. My clients have had the same experience, different blood types and all of my clients have noticed the benefits when they avoid the foods suggested to avoid by for their blood type.

The science behind the Blood Type Diet is all about antigens. Antigens are the chemical markers that determine your blood type. They form part of our chemical fingerprint by possessing a different antigen. Antigens are the body's internal security system – so when your immune system finds a foreign intruder (e.g. a foreign antigen from bacteria) it checks with your blood type antigen to see if it is friend or foreign object. The blood type diet seems most useful in knowing which foods to avoid rather than only sticking with the most beneficial foods.

This is because when the presence of dietary lectins, which consist of protein and are found in around 30 percent of food, they can be inhibited through cooking and digestion to some degree however if they reach the blood stream they can appear like foreign antigens interfering with digestion and absorption. They can also result in nutrient deficiencies, food allergies, arthritis/joint pain, irritability/mood swings, intestinal and digestive issues.

There are several reasons why I disagree with not following the Blood Type Diet exactly. First, when looking at various situations such as the amount of stress in ones life at a certain time in life they may require more protein, for example. Another reason, women my sense they require differing needs of proteins/carbohydrates/fats through out their monthly cycle. Lastly, a medical condition or a woman becomes pregnant, to name a few examples, the diet needs to be adjusted accordingly.

Right Type of Carbohydrate+Lean Protein+the Right Type & Amount of Fat+Hydration=One Uber Being!

You can see just how many different diets are out there. It can be confusing. I suggest doing your own reading, such as you are now and coming up with your own ratio. I am happy to give you these guidelines and share with you what has worked for me, as well as several of my clients.

As I mentioned early, through my research and experiments, I have come across the right nutrition plan that provides me with optimal energy, health and overall well being. It allows me to feel energized, yet calm, focused and healthy to be my Uber best in life.

In order to feel and think your Uber best, adequate nutrition is essential. If you are not eating the right foods, your muscles may not be properly fueled and also your brain may not be properly nourished to think clearly and make smart choices in life. As a result, your body may not be working at its full potential, which can lead to fatigue, dehydration, or low blood sugar as you go about your day. This is sometimes called "hitting the wall". And we need to eat the right foods that make us feel good-that allow us to feel and be our best, in all areas of our life.

An essential component to Tier One of your Uber Empowerment Lifestyle Plan should involve experimenting with different types of foods and drinks to learn what works best for you. We are all individuals and therefore have different preferences and digestive systems. For example, some people cannot tolerate solid foods within 3 hours prior to exercising, while others find that their performance is improved when they eat a carbohydrate-rich snack 1.5 hours before their workout. The important thing is to learn what foods you best tolerate, when to eat them, and how much to eat. With this knowledge you will have peace of mind that you are well prepared.

To provide you with an example, the Nutrition area on my Uber Empowerment Lifestyle Plan includes four major goals of proper nutrition daily in order to feel and think my Uber best. They are the following:

A. Making sure my muscles are adequately fueled

B. Prevent dehydration – stay hydrated

C. Prevent low blood sugar (hypoglycemia)

D. Ensuring that my entire body, especially my brain, receives the fuel and nutrients it needs for optimal functioning.

What are your goals for creating your unique nutritional plan that will help you feel and think your best? I would like you to write these down on your Uber Empowerment Lifestyle Plan.

Best Carbs For feeling Your Uber Self

The right carbohydrate will provide a wonderful source of energy, fiber vitamins and minerals. Carbohydrates can also provide important food components such as bioflavonoids, isoflavones and polyphenols.

I mentioned earlier the Low Glycemic Index Diet, I would suggest referring to that chart for the type of carbohydrate and use it accordingly. For example, if it is close to the time you will be working out, choose a medium to high glycemic index food along with a small portion of lean protein.

The Right Protein Supplement Choice To Include In Your Uber Nutrition Empowerment Plan

Protein is an important component to have in the diet. Protein is necessary for skin, muscle, hair and the tissues in our body. Protein is important for hormones and enzymes that help aid in digestion, metabolism and recovery for tissue.

High quality protein is the best such as found in fish, lean meats, nuts eggs, legumes and beans. Many times, adding a high quality protein powder into your diet can be very beneficial.

Protein Powder Drinks

There are various different types of protein sources for protein shakes. The best way to find which one you feel your best at, is to try the different ones. I find that egg white protein and also a high quality rice protein works best for me. Also, on occasion, I have a high quality whey protein shake. You may find that whey or soy protein works best for you. I suggest you choose a high quality protein regardless to which type of protein powder you choose. I would also highly suggest finding a protein powder with no artificial sweeteners and try to avoid sugar alcohol as well. Many of these types of high quality protein powders I would suggest visiting your local holistic pharmacy. These types of pharmacies have highly educated staff members, many who have a background in medical or homeopathic fields.

One thing I would like to discuss briefly is Soy Protein. Soy is nature's only plant source with all eight essential amino acids and a denser source of protein than any other bean. It is low in cholesterol and saturated fat, high in fiber, calcium, magnesium, and vitamin B6. In a healthy Asian diet, soy is a staple. Soy is a key ingredient in many infant formulas. A 1999 FDA ruling, allows manufacturers can state that 25 grams of soy protein a day may reduce heart disease. Soy has high levels of isoflavones, called phyto-estrogens. Phyto-estrogens are a weaker form of estrogen thought to interfere with the body's natural hormone levels. Typically, soy products contain between five and fifty milligrams of isoflavones per serving. So, I would suggest including soy in the diet, because of all of its benefits however, the key would be choosing a high quality soy protein powder and the soy foods in moderation. If you were to take a look at Asia, women have a lower rate of breast cancer and men have a lower rate of prostate cancer than the Western population. A woman in Japan, might have a few ounces of tofu in her soup at lunch, a man in China might have a handful of soy nuts in a day. These amounts of soy are beneficial and harmless. Some Americans on the other hand, have gone overboard with Soy and have included an intake of Soy from supplements, bars and shakes – too much per day. Soy pills are not really necessary and I would suggest eating one or two servings of soy foods a day or a high quality soy based protein powder/shake a day. For those who can feel better using Soy Protein than whey or rice protein, I think soy foods remain an excellent protein source along with eggs, nuts and a healthy, low-glycemic index diet.

How much (or too little) of isoflavones to consume per day? According to the *Center for Science in the Public Interest*, the chart below is a good guide to keep in mind for just how many isoflavones per day.

Food	Isoflavones
Meatless patties	*Less than 5 mg*
Cereals	*5 to 25 mg*
Soy Milk	*5 to 50 mg*
Veggie Burger	*5 to 10 mg*
Tofu	*15 to 30 mg*
Yogurt	*20 to 30 mg*
Grande Soy Latte	*30 to 55 mg*
Edamame	*35 mg*
Soy Nuts	*35 mg*

I would suggest limiting your intake of isoflavones to fewer than 70 milligrams per day. The chart above is a good guide because isoflavones are not listed on the nutrition labels and amounts vary widely based on processing.

The Right Fats Help To Feel Uber

Which ever nutrition plan you create, you must include the right type of fats and the right amount of fats you will need for your individual needs. Low fat is not necessarily healthy. Eating the right amount of fat, for you and the right type of fat is the key. The right type of fat can help you feel full faster and decrease your appetite, which may help you control the amount of food you eat. This can help you make smart and healthy food choices. Did you know that most fats are considered to be low glycemic index foods? This is just one reason why moderate fat intake can be good for you. Keep in mind it is the type of fat that can benefit you or NOT benefit you. Saturated fats from red meat and dairy can actually worsen insulin resistance and these are the exact type of fasts that can lead to sluggishness and many health problems. A high quality type of fat such as those found in olive oil, fish, flax seeds can actually improve your skin, immune system, and the way your body processes sugar and insulin. Best of all, the right type of fat in the right amount can help reduce the risk to many common diseases. To give you an idea of the good fats you can choose to add into your diet and the ones to avoid here is a list:

Good Fats to Choose	Fats to Avoid
Avocados	Cakes, cookies, pastries
Fish – such as cod, salmon, tuna	Potato chips
Flaxseed oil	Deep-friend foods
Nuts & nut butters	Margarine
Olive oil	Cheese
Seeds – such as pumpkin, sunflower	Trans fats such as "partially hydrogenated" oils
	Shortening and lard

Foods, Beverages & Supplement Included In My Uber Empowerment Lifestyle Plan

I will give you an example of the foods my Uber Empowerment Lifestyle Plan includes. When I stick with the foods that make me feel good, I also notice I feel more balanced, my blood sugar is balanced and I feel calm but energized.

Foods I eat that allow me to feel my best:

- Organic/skinless & grilled or baked: lean red meats, turkey, chicken (skinless), seafood, lamb
- Organic vegetables and fruits
- Raw nuts
- Protein powder (alternate between whey, egg white protein)
- Protein bars (low glycemic)
- Eggs and egg whites

Beverages:

- High alkaline water
- Green tea
- Regular coffee (two cups per day)
- Wine (in moderation)

Nutritional Supplements (Daily):

A high quality:

- Multivitamin
- Omega 3's (EPA-DHA) soft-gels
- Pro-biotic
- CoQ10 60-100 mg

I avoid most foods that have flour, wheat, corn, sugar, hard alcohol, beer. I am very selective about sauces, in fact, I usually prefer to cook with herbs. However, one option is to have sauce on the side and use sparingly. I try to keep wine in moderation. Moderation for myself is one or two glasses a few nights of the week, followed by zero a few nights of the week. The artificial sweeteners have no benefit for your health. I use Stevia as a natural sweetener from time to time. Stevia is a natural herb.

This is what has worked for me. If you find you are already on a nutrition plan very similar to this and still feeling sluggish, have unexplained symptoms, I would visit your doctor. Or you might want to consider, for optimal well-being, to visit either a CCN Certified Clinical Nutritionist or a MD at a holistic wellness clinic for complete testing that involves a thorough evaluation of laboratory tests. Some of the tests might include a vitamin deficiency test, basic and extended blood tests that check hormones, lipid, inflammatory and metabolic markers, DEXA bone scan, mental chronometric test, muscle strength, CV Profiler, antioxidant scan, and body composition evaluation.

These type of tests can help you find out if you are gluten sensitive or perhaps you are feeling sluggish and your hormones are out of balance causing you to have foggy thinking. Maybe you just need to go through a detox program?

Some people actually walk around inflamed, with fluid, toxins and antigens and other harmful substances and this is from eating the wrong foods for their blood type, metabolic makeup, or not the right ratio of protein and carbohydrates and fat for their sport or their lifestyle demands. Empower yourself to experiment and see which foods might assist with a good feeling for your body and which might make you not feel so well. This is where we are all different. To save you time, as I mentioned earlier, you could go through a series of tests to find out which foods you are sensitive to, allergic to or if you have a vitamin deficiency or hormonal imbalance.

Balanced Thoughts On Eating

Looking at the body and choosing the right nutrients for each individual is a true art. Food IS medicine to our bodies and our health:

> *"The wise man should consider that health is the greatest*
> *of human blessings. Let food be your medicine."*
> *- Hippocrates*

As you can see, there are many diets out there and many factors to take into consideration, like your metabolic type, blood type, your fitness goals in wanting to gain weight or loose weight, your desire to feel more energetic and to think with clarity. I touched on each of these factors briefly, in order to provide you with some guidelines in assisting you in creating your own nutrition plan, not just some diet plan, as part of your Uber Empowerment Lifestyle Plan. You can choose to take what works for you in each of the nutrition plans mentioned above-some of the suggestions in the metabolic type may make more sense to you and some of the suggestions you may want to blend from knowing more about your blood type, which foods cause you to become congested or cause you inflammation (usually these are dairy, wheat, sugar, refined carbohydrates, and for some people even grains). Which foods make you feel sluggish, irritable. Keep a daily journal of what you eat, portion size, and how you feel each day for at least a week, if not up to a month. As you change your lifestyle choices, you will need patience before seeing dramatic transformation. Everyone is at a different level in life. You may realize how much better you feel in just a few days to a week or you may not notice a difference in how you feel until a month, sometimes up to three months.

It does not have to feel overwhelming to make these choices. Keeping track choosing a lean, high quality protein, the right type of carbohydrate (a choice from the low glycemic index chart) and a good fat choice, does not have to feel overwhelming.

At first, you'll want to empower yourself by keeping track of this – usually done best by writing this down in a journal. And soon, this becomes a natural habit. You will intuitively, know what your body needs to feel at its best. You will intuitively make positive healthy lifestyle choices. You will know what to choose to eat for a long, hectic day and for a non-active day. You may realize you feel your Uber Best when you eat every 3 to 4 hours instead of every 2 hours.

It is important to feel balanced and have healthy thoughts on eating. My hope is that all of this information on eating and nourishing your body with positive protocols will be a wonderful guide for you – a guide that you can take and tweak to meet your needs, if you need to. Come up with what works for you. This is your pace and your ratio that will allow you to achieve your Uber Self through out your day and life. I'm sharing with you what has worked for me, in hopes you'll find the true you.

By adjusting your caloric intake to match expenditure, you will continue to feel empowered and inner connected to what your personal needs are. Keep in mind your body requires energy to perform workouts. It is with the right lean protein plus the right effective carbohydrates (chosen from the low glycemic index chart) and the right type of fat.

You have a strong desire or goal right now. Whatever will help you to feel your Uber Best, I believe we are all given a body and we should take the best care of it – yet also still be able to live a realistic life and be sane about it. It does take motivation and true desire and commitment and discipline.

I also believe that goals should be realistic and something we can truly live with and be sane about. A suggestion would be to commit to where you want to "be" and get there and then live an 80% to 20% life. This means, 80% of the time (lets say during the week, as an example) you are good, 100% committed to the foods and beverages you've listed on your Uber Empowerment Lifestyle Plan under Nutrition and Optimal Wellness. The weekends would be the 20%. You are not outrageous, yet you enjoy. This might be a realistic and ideal lifestyle and I also think that if you are surrounded by others who can support or believe in what you do, of course this will only help.

To sum all of this up, you can keep it simple.

Nutrition is pretty basic at its core: eat more fruit and vegetables, lean protein and fish; eat fewer chips and cheeseburgers. But you have so many options these days that they can confuse you. Here are some simple tips that will make eating easier:

1. Make drinking into a habit.

    I know you know by now that you should drink eight
    250 ml glasses of water a day, and even more if you're
    very active and train extra hard. So make it simple:
    keep a two-liter water bottle on your desk, and ensure
    that you drain it by the end of your work day. (Then
    request a desk closer to the toilets!) Important: type
    of water you drink is very, very important. DO NOT

drink tap water. I suggest doing a bit of research in this area so you feel comfortable making your selection on water. In my experience, I have noticed I feel and think my best when I drink a more alkaline type of water. You can find alkaline water through various manufactures. I suggest making some time to research and see which type of ionized water machine will meet your needs. I like the following: Fiji Water when traveling, Kangen water system for home use. This can be an investment – your health is worth it. It all starts with what we put into our mouth whether it is food or beverage.

2. Snacks – so you can be feel your Ultimate Uber Self all day long.

A famished person after their workout or after working all day and not having eaten a healthy lunch, typically makes poor food choices. I've seen very hungry people tend to eat fast food, and not fruit and vegetables that help to protect health. So keep your appetite satisfied with several light, healthy snacks throughout the day.

These are healthy choices, however they should be chosen selectively and only one to two of these choices per day, on an active day. They are healthy and include healthy fat, however the calories are high and so they should be limited as one per day on a non-active day. Take into consideration your caloric needs based on how active your day is...

Best Choice – all nuts have a benefit. All are high in good fats. Some nuts have more magnesium than others (cashews) and some more calcium or iron (Almonds are high up on the list for this). Peanuts have more resveratrol than grapes. So the key with nuts is – mix them up! Eat a variety of them. Be mindful of portion size with them. A handful a day is very beneficial for the heart and many other health benefits.

Organic nuts – raw almonds, raw walnuts, raw pumpkin seeds, also raw almond butter, soy nut butter, peanut butter (unsweetened and low carbohydrates) – I would suggest raw and a brand that has no hydrogenated oils.

3. Low-Carbohydrates or Low Glycemic index Protein Bars are a good choice as well.

    Although they tend to be high in calories and fat, they often are better than a slice of pizza or a candy bar at the airport.

4. Lower Calorie Treats.

    Fruit: Apples, pears and grapes are durable, and almost any other fruit can be stored in a container. So keep in mind these fruit are also good choices: plums, blueberries, strawberries, raspberries, peaches. There are many to choose from. Variety is key – seasonal selection can help keep your appetite satisfied. Raw vegetables or even pre-cooked/steamed vegetables are a very healthy choice.

Is all of this sounding overwhelming to you? Does it feel as if this is going to be difficult for you? Okay, then now would be a great time to pull out your journal and review your Uber Self Improvement list (you DID create that list I told you to right?!) of why you want to be feel your Uber Best. Review this. Review it again. Do you agree with what you wrote? Maybe you have even more reasons now of why you want to finally feel your best. The reasons again, for me are: when I follow my Uber Empowerment Lifestyle Plan, I feel balanced, energetic, less mood swings and much more loving towards others, toward myself and toward life. And an added benefit from true commitment toward eating healthy is you will feel and think your best.

Your Uber Self & Your Physical Body Begins To Change & Show Positive Results

You will begin to feel better and think more clearly when you follow your nutrition plan. Another positive result will be – you'll look even better. When we feel out best in the inside, this will show through to others – our inner being at its best is non-stoppable! I once read somewhere, that the best beauty potent is inside of us, this could be our inner confidence, our sense of peace within us that we carry around with us throughout the day and others are drawn to you, even strangers. When we physically feel our best, our spirituality is in a higher connection with us and can emulate greater distance. This is your Uber Self, you can rely on and call upon when you most need it.

Physically, you will feel stronger and lighter, you'll have increased energy. One of the most healthy things you can do for your body, in regards to body composition, is loose inches, but gain LEAN muscle, so if you have a "fixation" on the number on the scale, try to change your perspective on that. Lean muscle weighs heavier than fat. This can be a real mental challenge sometimes for some because they tend to think the lighter they are in weight, the faster they will be on the trails and in the next race. Yes and no. Yes, it is good to keep your body weight on the lighter side, yet it is always best to stay in the range of your ideal body weight. We all have a body weight range where we feel and look our best AND think our best. The more connected we are to ourselves and have an inner awareness of our body's needs-physically, mentally, emotionally and spiritually and taking care of these needs all the time – being consistent with self-care-then we will make positive, healthy choices each day – throughout our day, every hour, every second, every heartbeat at a time.

Key to remember is the ratio of calorie input needs to support the energy out put. You notice days will fluctuate depending on energy/activity out put. Rest days (a non-workout day) are important from training and on those rest days your nutrition needs will change slightly. You won't need as many carbohydrate grams that day or protein grams that day or even as much fat grams on a rest day. (Below you will find the Harris Benedict Formula-I have found this to be a great tool in determining my nutrition based on my daily activity factor).

We need to think of nutrition as a workout partner and brain fuel for daily life. It's a powerful means to fuel you to perform well and enhance your workout recovery, yet too many people in life ignore the importance of fueling their engines with quality foods.

If you don't give your body the fuel it needs, it becomes catabolic, drawing fuel from your lean muscle — the very thing you've worked so hard to create. Proper post-workout nutrition is essential as it restores your body's hormonal equilibrium and jump starts repair and recovery.

Your body requires energy to perform workouts. The main thing to keep in mind is your caloric intake must match your activity level on a day to day basis, not only for maintaining the weight you are currently at, if that is the weight you wish to maintain, but also if you are wanting to shed a few pounds. Your caloric intake is also important to match your day to day activity level so you will have optimal energy, healthy immune response, and managing stress. There are many different formulas you can use to figure out how many calories you should consume a day based on how many calories you are expending. I like the Harris Benedict Formula. Below is a guideline you can use to figure your activity level.

Harris Benedict Formula

To determine your total daily calorie needs, multiply your <u>BMR</u> by the appropriate activity factor, as follows:

1. If you are sedentary (little or no exercise):
   Calorie-Calculation = BMR x 1.2

2. If you are lightly active (light exercise/sports 1-3 days/week): Calorie-Calculation = BMR x 1.375

3. If you are moderately active (moderate exercise/sports 3-5 days/week): Calorie-Calculation = BMR x 1.55

4. If you are very active (hard exercise/sports 6-7 days/week): Calorie-Calculation = BMR x 1.725

5. If you are extra active (very hard exercise/sports & physical job or 2x training): Calorie-Calculation = BMR x 1.9

Total Calorie Needs Example
If you are sedentary, multiply your BMR (1745) by 1.2 = 2094. This is the total number of calories you need in order to maintain your current weight.

Once you know the number of calories needed to maintain your weight, you can easily calculate the number of calories you need to eat in order to gain or lose weight:

Calorie Needed To Lose Weight

There are approximately 3500 calories in a pound of stored body fat. So, if you create a 3500-calorie deficit through diet, exercise or a combination of both, you will lose one pound of body weight. (On average 75% of this is fat, 25% lean tissue) If you create a 7000 calorie deficit you will lose two pounds and so on. The calorie deficit can be achieved either by calorie-restriction alone, or by a combination of fewer calories in (diet) and more calories out (exercise). This combination of diet and exercise is best for lasting weight loss. Indeed, sustained weight loss is difficult or impossible without increased regular exercise.

If you want to lose fat, a useful guideline for lowering your calorie intake is to reduce your calories by at least 500, but not more than 1000 below your maintenance level. For people with only a small amount of weight to lose, 1000 calories will be too much of a deficit. As a guide to minimum calorie intake, the American College of Sports Medicine (ACSM) recommends that calorie levels never drop below 1200 calories per day for women or 1800 calories per day for men. Even these calorie levels are quite low.

An alternative way of calculating a safe minimum calorie-intake level is by reference to your body weight or current body weight. Reducing calories by 15-20% below your daily calorie maintenance needs is a useful start. You may increase this depending on your weight loss goals.

For additional information, you can also use to figure your activity level:

http://www.bmi-calculator.net/bmr-calculator/harris-benedict-equation/

Nutritional Supplements

There are way too many Nutritional Supplements out there on the market today, wouldn't you agree? And so which Nutritional Supplements are actually needed in a person's diet, when this person is already consistent with a foundational diet that includes a low glycemic index diet and they are including high quality fish oil (EPA-DHA), along with a high quality multivitamin? I have experienced certain nutritional supplements that can be very effective in providing key nutrients for a stressful lifestyle and a very active lifestyle. I also have realized which nutritional supplements can be key nutrients for building a solid immune response in myself, as well as assisting me with endurance and stamina in my workouts.

I have experienced the following nutritional supplements that can be key nutrients for stress: Pantothenic Acid, Vitamin C (1,000 ml), B6, Zinc and Magnesium. You can also get many of these nutrients in foods such as green vegetables for magnesium, fish and chicken for B6, and for pantothenic Acid, salmon is a good choice. And of course including EPA-DHA in a high quality supplement is also something I would suggest.

The Nutritional Supplements that can be key nutrients for very active people are: EPA-DHA to maintain lean muscle, fight inflammation, cardiovascular health improvement. The American Heart Association has stated just one gram of fish oil per day for healthy cardiovascular health and for maintenance. I have increased my EPA-DHA up to 2 to 4 grams a day, when I needed an anti-inflammatory. And it DOES work! You just have to use enough OF the EPA-DHA. I would also suggest a high quality multivitamin for good energy production and immune system function, nerve and muscle function. This will assure to cover all of your nutritional bases. If you're already eating a balanced diet, this should give you extra insurance. Calcium for strong bones, Magnesium for assisting in calcium absorption and may even increase bone density. Magnesium is also important for healthy heart beat and lower blood pressure. Both Vitamin C and Vitamin E are also a great supplement to your protocol. The Vitamin C works as an antioxidant and works well with Vitamin E to protect our joint tissue from the degradation that often can occur in arthritic conditions. CoQ10, Coenzyme Q10—This nutrient is vital for every organ in our bodies, especially our heart. It has many beneficial qualities and one of the most beneficial qualities would be how amazing an antioxidant it can be in cardiovascular health. Our body levels of CoQ10 will naturally decline as we age. Research shows a CoQ10 supplement can really benefit athletes, as well as most over age 35. For painful inflammation, Glucosamine, MSM and Chondroitin Sulfate can reduce inflammation and enhance flexibility as well as help to maintain healthy joint cartilage. I also like to supplement with ALA, Alpha Lipoic Acid. ALA functions as a co-factor for energy production and is also a powerful anti-oxidant that can help combat free radicals. Athletes are quite aware that exercise increases oxidative stress on the body and the need for antioxidant protections. What is not known too well is that intense training can cause oxidative damage to red blood cells.

One other area to consider for very active people and individuals who live stressful lives, are the adrenals. There are both excellent herbs on the market for this as well as a nutritional support type formula. I suggest looking for herbs such as Cordyceps, Rhodiaola Root Extract, and Asian Ginseng Root Extract. For a nutritional support formula for adrenals look for Vitamin B6, Riboflavin, Pantothenic-Acid, raw adrenal concentrate – bovine, and para-aminobenzoic acid. As I mentioned previously in this chapter, a great place to find such formulas and herbs as well as high quality vitamins and supplements is to visit a local holistic type pharmacy.

Never start taking any supplements without first checking with your doctor.

Nourishing Your Uber Soul

Another thing to keep in mind, as I discussed earlier, emotional eating- sometimes leads to the wrong type of foods and that can make us feel low energy, depressed, sluggish and unloving toward others, toward ourselves and toward life. Remember, to feed your soul each day as well as your physical body-reach for that favorite inspirational book that opens up your heart to love and joy and reminds you how beautiful life is.

Keep reading the inspirational resource that speaks to your soul each day. Some of my clients find that reading quotes form their favorite leader or favorite athlete nourishes their hunger, uplifts and motivates them to reach their Uber Self. And for some of us, it could be reading a book on positive affirmations. And others it is the Bible. Whatever inspirational source feeds YOUR soul the most, keep reading it each day. Our souls need to be nourished each day, just as much as we feed and nourish our physical body and minds.

I have found the following books to be inspirational and provide self-growth:

"It's Time To Get Selfish" – Robyn Busfield

"If Life is a Game, These are the Rules" – Cherie Carter-Scott, PH.D

"10 Secrets for Success and Inner Peace" – Dr. Wayne Dyer

"The Right Questions" – Debbie Ford

"The Four Agreements" – Don Miguel Ruiz

"The Three Keys to Self-Empowerment" – Stuart Wilde

I suggest to my clients to stay in contact with like minded people and share inspirational knowledge and choose to include in your reading, personal growth and professional development related topics. Many of my clients find it helps to keep an updated "Suggested Reading List".

The science behind nutrition is certainly appreciated but nothing can empower you more than your own intuition with which foods are good for your own individual body and which foods are bad for your body. Listen to your body – never under estimate what it is trying to tell you. Your Intuition can be your most Powerful Source if you allow it to be AND to trust it.

We have discussed how to use intuition and mindfulness to help you create your individual nutrition plan as part of Tier One of your Uber Empowerment Lifestyle Plan. The remainder of Tier One on your Uber Empowerment Lifestyle Plan, will be discussed in the next two chapters. Let's now take a look at how Uber Energetic Movement® can empower you to choose the best exercise for your mind, body and soul.

Please also be advised that my experiences and my opinions and the references cited are for information only, and are not intended to diagnose or prescribe. For your specific diagnosis and treatment, consult your doctor or health care provider.

***Note: I encourage everyone to see a doctor before altering their diet, taking a supplement and/or performing athletic, fitness or other strenuous physical activity. It is your responsibility to evaluate the accuracy, completeness and usefulness of any information, instruction, opinion or advice contained in the content.

CHAPTER 3

Uber Energetic Movement® For Mind, Body And Soul

"True Spirituality is a mental attitude you can practice at anytime"
- Dalai Lama

I think the most valuable tools I can share with you, is the fact that both your intuition and mind set have to be there to choose the right nutrition and the right form of exercise to help you feel and think your Uber Best. Your attitude, your positive thoughts, to believe in yourself – know who you are, know what you want to achieve, your inner beliefs. Consistency and persistence and learning to stay inner connected, in tune to each need you have and listening to that whispered wisdom and follow it, each day, every second, every hour, every breath, every heartbeat at a time.

It can be more challenging on some days, but with consistency and a commitment to yourself, you can do it. It is a test of ultimate will, fully utilizing your own Uber Empowerment Lifestyle Plan and when you strive to reach your Uber Self, you will feel empowered and most of all a powerful, inner-spiritual awareness that you are connected to your core beliefs and have the flexibility and balance to live with whatever life may have in store for you each day. All the technical information out there will not guarantee that you will feel your best on one specific diet or "cookie cut" plan. There just is not a One-Size-Fits-All-Plan. It is your opportunity to create your own Uber Empowerment Lifestyle Plan that works for YOU and to use the information I have shared with you as a guide.

In addition to choosing the right nutrition for yourself to feel and think your Uber Best, choosing the right form of exercise is important as well. I truly believe we are meant to enjoy exercise and that the most effective way to enjoy exercise is to view exercise in a more Holistic way. Exercise that allows creative and effective movement. This requires movement that feels good along with effective results that allows you to be in the flow – mentally, physically and connects you to your soul. When we include our spirituality and mental focus into our physical workouts and through all areas of our life, each day, this makes every moment more meaningful, enriches each encounter, and leads to quality of life. This is putting our heart and soul into each run, each workout and all activities – not just from a cardiovascular perspective-but also spiritual and with an openness to life, with an open heart. It is all connected. And you just might realize, when applying mind, body and soul, you feel less pain and less negative energy. You will feel Uber energized.

I urge you to begin to practice a more holistic method for exercise and observe how you feel, on all levels: physically, mentally and your soul. If the thought of exercise or fitness has never motivated you or hearing the words "workout", "exercise", "get fit", you might want to think of how you can move your body to allow you to experience feeling Uber energized. I have created the term Uber Energetic Movement® and this allows me to get creative with various exercises that connect my mind, body and soul and to feel empowered. Our bodies need movement. Movement helps to energize, center, focus, calm and release stress. The right Uber Energetic Movement® for you will empower you.

Uber Energetic Movement® defined:

> *Movement that has four components: mind-to-movement, aerobic, strength and flexibility; each of these four components can be used on its own or in any combination of the others, to create an overall feeling of energized, centered, focused and calm that connects your body, mind and soul.*

Remember this always – exercise should NOT hurt. Pain is NOT part of the aging process, you are not "getting older". Exercise may seem to hurt and be painful or boring, if you are over training and staying stuck in the same old routine day after day, year after year. I have found the most effective results allow me to experience fulfillment and balance when I mix things up.

Uber Energetic Movement® Has 4 Components

I will discuss each one of these areas: Mind-to-Movement, Aerobic, Strength and Flexibility. Each one of these areas is important for an overall, complete exercise program.

<u>Mind-to-Movement</u>

I would like to discuss this exercise component first. When I suggest to my clients to consider adding in a new perspective to really get involved and make the most out of each workout, by applying a more *inner awareness* side to exercise, they learn to embrace exercise with a whole new and positive approach.

I include mind-to-movement in my fitness plan, especially when I train solo. This allows me to be more aware of how I learn, grow and expand when I train solo. I am able to incorporate inner awareness with a mind set and focus into my run, my workout and my stretching session. Mind-to-movement has assisted me in preparing for a race, maintaining a healthy and fit body and soul, and prepared me for my day ahead so that I replenish my cup and I can continue to give to others with a loving heart and hand.

Most of my clients have told me they notice a sense of fulfillment in their day to day events. I encourage you to try this for a week or two and notice the new quality of time in your days and how it feels to live a quality life. If you have felt dissatisfaction in your life, your job, your workouts seem pointless even though you may already be eating healthy, mixing up your workouts to keep from becoming bored and to minimize injuries, it may be time to look within and pay more attention to how you are moving your body.

For example, how you are running. How would you like to see your body perform? Tell yourself why you are moving your body the way you are and why this sport is a creative part of you. Does this sport help you become confident in other areas of your life? Maybe it is teaching you a philosophy you have on life or this sport continues to show you new strategic planning ideas you can use in other areas of your life. But without implementing Mind-to-Movement into your sport, exercise and your day, something will not feel right. It could be injury from overuse, too many hours put in at work or a health problem at some point our bodies will communicate to us that something is out of alignment and something does not feel right both physically and mentally. This is when many of us become confused with our body's signals and our choices we've made in developing our lifestyle plan that seems to have worked so well for us for so many years that we come to a halt and just give up or stop the activities and interests we use to love. This may be the perfect time to look at things from a new perspective: a challenging situation may be an opportunity to reconstruct the body as a Whole. This revelation can lead us to develop Mind-to-Movement in our chosen sport or exercise so it feels natural, effortless and brings us more happiness and balance in our lives.

Get connected to how your body moves while working out, running, swimming, surfing, walking, weight-training. All types of exercise can promote a deep inner connection when your mind is inside the muscles, tissues, skeletal structure communicating to them to move in the way you want them to. This is how Mind-to-Movement feels.

I think running, yoga, weight training, walking and *all* exercise can offer a philosophy to it, a new spiritual way of embracing exercise, a way of living and moving in our bodies that it feels good, natural and effortless and we see effective results and most of all a type of exercise that makes us feel happy. Mind and conscience work together on sending signals to our feelings and our feelings help us become aware of how this movement or exercise makes us feel in this moment, right now. Noticing that movement and how the movement feels can be very enlightening. I was enlightened by mind-to-movement and which Uber Energetic Movement® felt good to me, when I was able to go for a brisk walk, with my music, right after an injury I had. Just being able to move my whole body once again, brought me happiness mentally and physically and I felt more balanced. I learned it is nice to do a physical activity with the right mind-set and that it brings me improvement on my body and feeling a more inner awareness. I can experience this through various ways of creative movement such as weight training and running, walking, stretching – with the right atmosphere, music and putting Mind to Movement.

Any creative movement done with the right mental focus and movement can support an overall sense of well being. This is one of my all time favorite motivators. Really, this is something I don't know about you, but

I need to remind myself this often – we all tend to get in a rush during our workouts, runs, swims and our forms then get very sloppy and the whole benefit and idea of being healthy and fit is gone.

I think this can go hand in hand with how sometimes we need to remind ourselves that we just need to focus on doing our best in our sport and in life. Sometimes going after the reward is not going to make us happy. But it is the action that is going to make us feel intensely happy, for much longer. When we want to do our best, we take action. And doing our best is taking action because we love it, not because we are expecting a reward/medal. Many people do the opposite. They only take action when they expect a reward, and they don't enjoy the action. And that is the reason why they don't do their best. For example, people that work just for payday. They are working for a reward, and as a result they resist work. They try to avoid the action and it becomes more difficult, and they don't do their best.

Looking at a sport we love and in all areas of our life, we need to use mind-to-movement, do our best. Focus on *your* best. Avoid self-suffering. And when you focus on your best-you will feel more fulfilled and intensely happy with your overall performance. Not comparing yourself to others. Action is what makes the difference and taking the best care of your body. Empower yourself to have a strong self-love for yourself and your body and to respect your body by making healthy nutritional choices and allow your body to rest and heal and exercise and do what makes your body feel good.

I would like to ad that although I have discussed adding Mind-to-Movement during those workouts when you train solo, Mind-to-Movement can offer some great insight as well, in group and team sports or when working out with a partner if you allow it to be.

Mind-to-Movement will open up exactly what each individual needs to learn at that time, that moment of inner awareness – through each workout. Now that we know the meaning of Mind to Movement, let's use this new perspective in all of the other three areas of Uber Energetic Movement®: Aerobic/Endurance, Strength and Flexibility.

Aerobics For Uber Endurance

Progressively increase the intensity in the aerobic area of your Uber Energetic Movement®. Intensity comes into focus in all three of these areas, especially with the Aerobic and Strength areas. It is important to increase intensity gradually.

(Example: Even a 12 year old cannot snowboard 3 days in a row without some type of unhealthy stress on the knees!!).

Intensity Terms:

- Easy Effort: Active recovery, approximately 50-67% of maximum heart rate.

- Moderate Effort: Aerobic Endurance, 68-79% of maximum heart rate.

- Higher Effort: Approximate lactate threshold or sustained race pace, 80-89% of maximum heart rate.

Variety in life, keeps us flexible and open to seeing new perspectives to our day to day events that come up. Vary your runs, walks, cardiovascular exercises – the terrain, types of intensity and endurance. Some examples:

1. Hills – they build strength in your legs. Believe it or not, your legs will not become as fatigued as fast as they do pounding the pavement over and over on flat, long runs and walks, especially on concrete. Rolling hills are great and more of a complete workout/run. It is best to do these on alternating days, or spread them out over several days, mixed with shorter and flat runs. What other "hills" or "mountains" would you like to reach the top of today?

2. Grass/Trails/dirt paths – a different surface feels great and your body will thank you. The change of scenery will keep you inspired too.

3. Track – at a high school or a college. Your body will thank you on this as well for a mix up of different terrain. Not as exciting, and so maybe use these track surfaces for speed workout, the pounding you'll be doing during this type of run session is best to do anyway on a track surface, or a treadmill.

4. Treadmill at gym – great for those days when you're traveling and not use to the environment/neighborhood you may be in. Also, certain days weather will permit you to be indoors.

5. Sand/beach runs – this will be a challenge for some of you. Thick sand can be a great leg workout! Miles will be shorter at first. It also can take awhile to build up pace. This type of running requires a different type of form and technique. The sand is not for everyone – if it does not feel right on your ankles, shins or hips or

the knees, then don't run in the sand. Others folks love the sand.

Yes, you can also choose to run on concrete/outdoors. However, when you run on dirt or other soft surfaces whenever possible, this is ideal to running on asphalt and especially concrete, this can result in greater muscular skeletal impact and can lead to injury.

Varying your runs and walks with other types of cardiovascular Uber Energetic Movement®, such as indoor cycling/spinning, outdoor cycling or bike ride (mountain bike or even a beach cruiser ride), the gym cardiovascular machines can also help minimize injuries and boredom. I vary my runs with other forms of cardiovascular movement such as using the rotating stair climber at the gym or indoor cycling.

Mixing up various forms of cardiovascular Uber Energetic Movement® is what can keep you from getting bored and hopefully prevent injuries. It will also help you mix up speed workouts, endurance workouts and strength/power workouts.

I have provided a schedule as an example, in Tier One, on the Uber Empowerment Lifestyle Plan in the resource section of this book, for achieving and maintaining aerobic endurance. You will see I listed various forms of cardiovascular type movements. You can feel free to mix and create your own combination of cardiovascular Uber Energetic Movement®. Certain days your plan may be for an easy cardiovascular session and keeping the pace steady and moderate and other days it could be more interval training where you include bursts of speed or higher intensity for a brief period in your workout, then allow your body to recover for a minute or two and repeat with another short burst of intensity.

This is a guideline for some structure to your cardiovascular activity schedule. Always listen to your body and if the suggested activity you have down for that particular day, does not sound like the best choice for you, consider all your options and all the possibilities of creative and effective Uber Energetic Movement® and select one. This could be your body's way of trying to communicate to you that it needs something new – yoga, dance, roller blade? Your body could also be trying to communicate to you that you are over training in that particular sport or activity and to choose an alternative. Cross-train by choosing at least two different types of cardiovascular exercises to perform on alternating days. It is always good to have some type of guideline though for motivation and showing any type of continued progress you might want to see.

The activities listed are for cardiovascular activities for 30-60 minutes. I prefer to do my cardiovascular activity in the morning and strength training sessions in the afternoon. This is what feels best to my body, however you may prefer to do your cardiovascular workouts in the afternoon or early evening.

Building Uber Strength

Some people prefer to do strength training sessions in the late afternoon to early evening because their muscles tend to respond better at this time of day. It can be very individual.

I have my strength training sessions broken down into 3 different muscle groups. I allow plenty of rest between the strength training sessions to avoid injury. Ideally, the key is to be consistent and try to stick with 2 to 3 different muscle groups on most weeks. Each strength training session is intense focus between 30 to 60 minutes, depending on which muscle groups are targeted for that session. For example, on a day when

I strength train arms and abs my time spent in the gym for that training session is 30-40 minutes. When I strength train lower body/legs I am in the gym between 45-60 minutes.

Cross train your strength sessions by using a combination of calisthenics, free weights, tubing and bands, machines. Cross training will reduce the risk of injury from repetitive strain and overuse. You can work some muscles while other muscles are recovering or resting.

The weekly schedule for performing two to three strength training sessions I have had success with, are divided into these 3 muscle groups:

- Shoulders/Triceps/Biceps
- Legs (quadriceps, hamstrings & calves)
- Chest/Biceps/Abs

I suggest allowing enough rest between sessions if your focus is on upper body that week, usually at least 48 hours between sessions is sufficient. You can use the same muscle group combination as a guide or create your own combination. Key is to remember to use a variety so your body does not get use to the same exercises over and over and this will also help to eliminate injuries.

You might want to experiment with various workouts. For example, I find I have better energy to split cardiovascular workouts from strength training sessions.

Depending on your schedule, you may find you need to include both cardiovascular and strength training sessions together during your time at the gym. As for strength training, also, listen to your body. The sets and reps and intensity I suggest are a guideline and what I try to be consistent with. There may be times where you allow your body not just one week of rest between the work out sessions per muscle group, but up to a week and a half. Usually, this will be because of the fact you may increase the intensity of weight you are lifting.

For someone just starting out with their strength training as well as those who have had recent injuries, these are things to take into consideration as how much you want to include in your training schedule. The guide I provided for you is what I did and has worked for me. I also have been running and doing various cardiovascular exercises for over 21 years, and consistently lifted weights for over 15 years. And even with all of this in mind, it is still all about listening to your body. Even though I have all these years of experience behind me, I also have to use my inner awareness to assess how I am feeling over all. Asking your self questions such as how has my sleep been over the last week and how can I get consistent good quality sleep each night or on a consistent basis. Other questions such as how is my energy level? Do I have good energy for work on the days I am working out? How is my apatite and am I being consistent with my nutrition choices? All of these and other questions will allow you to develop your own Uber Empowerment Lifestyle Plan as well as how often you can use my workout schedule when you are just striving for maintaining a healthy and fit body or trying to create one. This is part of creating your Tier One in your Uber Empowerment Lifestyle Plan.

The key to improving fitness is to gradually and progressively build duration and intensity. Our body absorbs the training and adapts by getting stronger during rest. I know to some of you this is going to be a challenge to get use to. I am one of those people while the rest of this world is trying to motivate them selves to roll out of bed and outside for their run/into the gym for their workout, I am trying to convince myself it is okay to take a rest day. I know now how important recovery workouts and complete rest are required to feel stronger, get faster and to feel well overall.

If you are going to strength train at a high intensity focus, I suggest taking a recovery week every fourth week. And this is not the time to pig out and go out partying. This is a recovery week where you allow yourself more sleep while still staying on your consistent sleep time schedule. (Go to bed ½ an hour earlier and/or sleeping a ½ hour later would be one example and not so extreme it will throw you off your sleep cycle). A recovery week is definitely lower intensity, slower pace, and fewer miles. Doing enough exercise to remind your muscles to stay fit, healthy, strong and lean.

I often suggest to my clients who are over age 40 may want to consider resting more often than younger people. I have suggested as well, to my clients who are over age 50, to consider scheduling a full recovery week every second or third week from strength training. Again, listen to your body. Your body gives you subtle and maybe not so subtle signs of taking a rest.

Let's take a look at repetitions and intensity and how you can tailor these tools to fit your Uber Energetic Movement® Plan.

Repetitions

Depending on your fitness goals, there are a variety of repetition ranges to achieve your Uber Energetic Movement® goals.

A strength training program focusing on 4 to 6 repetitions is best for increasing strength and power. This focus is toward power-lifting goals, due to the considered low repetition range.

A strength training program focusing on 8 to 12 repetitions is best for increasing overall muscularity and this is a focus toward creating a bodybuilding physique, because of the use of moderate repetition range.

A strength training program focusing on 15 to 20 repetitions is ideal for increasing definition and muscular hardness. This focus is on high repetition range and is to assist you in achieving that lean muscle tone. This is the focus I use and feel my best at. This is an area I find ideal-you can create from here. If you want to build a certain area lets say you want to build up your biceps, yet every other area you want to maintain and keep a lean muscle tone and definition. You would stick with the 15 to 20 reps for your entire body except the biceps. For this area, you would want to build and be consistent with 8 to 12 reps.

For the number of sets, I focus each week on implementing anywhere from 6 to 12 sets per muscle group, using two to four different exercises each workout. I like to use only a 20 to 30 second rest between sets, because focus is on definition.

To get a variety and always keep your body guessing, it can be fun, creative and effective to cycle phase your strength training sessions. This would include 3 phases. Each phase would last about 4 weeks. You could start with the Power Phase, this is the phase that suggests to 4 to 6 reps with longer rest periods in between each set. Great time to use Circuit Training during this phase to allow that five to seven minute rest in between sets. Remember, this type of low repetition is great for building power and strength.

In the second cycle phase, you would begin about four weeks after completing the phase one cycle. You would begin using 8-12 reps per exercise and allow about 30 seconds rest in between sets. Stick with this cycle phase for four weeks. This repetition cycle phase focuses on overall muscularity.

After four weeks of the second cycle phase, begin to focus your strength training sessions on higher repetition of 15-20. The shortest rest time in between sets is suggested, aim for between 20 to 30 seconds rest in between sets. This strength training cycle phase allows definition and hardness. After four weeks of this cycle phase, you could consider one week off from weights/strength training and then start up again with phase one.

You may find you prefer to consistently stick with the repetitions that work most effective for you. It is not necessary to cycle phase your strength sessions, but if you are looking for some variety, then it can help to get creative through cycle phasing.

Intensity

I suggest working up to failure on all sets. The range of reps I do is 15 to 20. At first you may barely get to rep 15. This is good. This means you are using heavy enough weight to build strength and definition. You have room to grow – you can increase the rep over time. You can also increase the amount of weight when you need to, over time. Another option is to perform a super-set in some of your weight training sessions. A super-set is performing 2 exercises in succession with no rest between sets. I have listed super-sets, to give you an idea. I like to keep a variety and I will do a super-set when I want to increase intensity or if I am short on time that day. Again, this is an option and you don't have to include super-sets into every weight-training session. This *will* increase the intensity of your workout and some days and weeks you may have the energy for this and other days and weeks you may need to really take into consideration how much intensity you really need in your weight training sessions, due to an upcoming race or maybe you have felt run down and need to lighten up the intensity this week. Listen to your body.

To give you an idea of how to combine different exercises to create a month of work out sessions where you do not use the same exercises week after week, what has proven to work well for me is to carry a small to medium size notebook that lists a variety of exercises per muscle group. I keep this notebook in my gym bag. I like to look it over right before I begin my workout.

Your time spent in the gym should be focused. You may have experienced a lot of time passing in the gym and you did not really focus or get what you would have liked to with your time spent in the gym. Remember, it is not how much time you spend in the gym it is the quality of your workout. I spend between 40 minutes up to 60 minutes each session. This is about 20 minutes per muscle group.

For example, 20 minutes for Back and 15 to 20 minutes for chest and about 10 to 15 minutes for abs. Being focused-Mind to Movement! – only resting between 20 to 30 seconds between sets, you should find this is plenty of time. You may want to use five minutes to warm up when you first get to the gym-a five minute walk on the treadmill at a slight incline or ride the bike for five minutes. Also, allowing yourself to stretch after your workout for 10-15 minutes will help your muscles recover more quickly and to lengthen them and stay flexible.

For a variety of exercises to apply in strength training or for a more creative approach, body sculpting, which is focusing on the areas of your body you most want to create definition, I would suggest compiling different exercises off of the internet, fitness magazines, and if you so desire, hiring a personal trainer for a period of time to keep your workouts mixed up.

I would suggest strength training a minimum of at least <u>every other day</u>, allowing a 48 hour rest in between sessions, on most days. This will help avoid injuries as well and with a 48 hour rest period will help with muscles recover more completely. Remember, you are creating a guide to follow for some motivation and structure. You may find you need to make some alterations to it that will help you feel YOUR Uber best.

You can choose to workout the same specific muscle groups, but try for a different combination of exercises each week, thus you have four different combinations per muscle group for your strength building/ body sculpting sessions. Feel free to mix and match exercises to fit your own needs. Certain exercises may not benefit you in designing the areas you want to build, you can change the intensity, reps and if a specific exercise does not feel right to you, then eliminate that exercise from your Uber Energetic Movement Plan. You get to create your own Uber Empowerment Lifestyle Plan by creating the Uber Energetic Movement exercises that feel the best to you, just as you created your individual nutrition plan in chapter two.

Flexibility For Uber Self

There's nothing wrong with stretching as long as it's done after a workout or on a less strenuous workout day. I would suggest implementing yoga postures into your stretching routine such as downward dog which will strengthen and stretch the feet, calves, hamstrings, gluts and opens up the upper back and shoulders, assisting in good posture as well as lengthening the muscles.

I also like child's pose for lower back and opening up the hip flexors and stretching the upper back. Traditional, classic stretches can also be used. By listening to your body and feeling where you are holding tightness, you will know which areas you need to stretch so you can minimize injuries and feel your best. If you have time in your schedule, you can include a Yoga class each week or be consistent with doing yoga poses at home for about 10 to 20 minutes a session, about three times a week. This makes a big difference in flexibility physically and mentally and great for your soul. And focusing on any tightness in my body and asking myself what am I holding onto and why and how can I gently release what is feeling tight or not right in my life so I can continue feel, think and be Uber Empowered. Remember, there is a lot to learn in Mind to Movement.

Just how intense should a stretch be to develop flexibility? Because intensity is based on subjective factors (tension, discomfort, pain), there is no way for me to determine this level for my clients; the intensity of the stretch must be up to you. In general, stretch to the point of tension but not pain.

People who are undergoing rehabilitation and have healing tissues, the point before pain is reached may be sufficient to rupture already weakened tissues. Remember, the best advice is to use common sense: Train, don't strain.

We are all at our own performance peak level and may be holding onto too many things in our own lives right now that are causing us to be less flexible in other areas of our life. It is important to keep our physical body flexible as well as our mental self, the mind. Stiffness can represent fear and fear can force us to hold onto things from the past or old ways of doing things and they are no longer useful for us.

A great example is, my client Jeff, who would run on the same exact route, everyday at the same time, at the same pace and same intensity and never increasing the miles or even mixing up the speed or intensity. Jeff saw this as one run, one way of doing a run. His body was holding stiffness in certain areas, in his hips and his knees-this stiffness was holding Jeff back in other areas of his life, not moving forward in life.

Another example of inflexibility or stiffness in the body, would be, lets say your neck is very stiff and you have very limited flexibility in your neck. Currently, in your career life, you have a situation with one of your top accounts. In the past, you had a similar experience with a different account. You took care of the situation and it was fixed. However, when a very similar experience came up again with a different account, you relied on that same old way and thought it would work this time, with this account. It didn't. That is holding on to one useful tool or way and hoping it will work all the time. Inflexibility in your neck can correlate with feelings of stubbornness. It is best to ease up and try to see challenges and situations from all perspectives. It is important to allow new creative ways to flow through us all the time and one way we can do this is to free up stiffness in the body and we can do this with mind-to-movement stretching which can help us become more flexible, physically and mentally. Life was meant to be creative and open up to new ideas, new perspectives, and try a new approach.

Improving and retaining flexibility depend on numerous variables, including genetic factors, age, and the state of training. Thus, your muscles' responses to regular stretching are a function of these factors and are dependent on which muscle group you stretch. Generally, for healthy individuals, the longer, more frequently, and more intensely you stretch, the faster and more significant your improvement in flexibility will be. If you are healthy, uninjured, and just starting a stretching program, you may feel increased muscle tightness and some muscle soreness the first week. But as your body adapts to regular stretching, you'll begin to see increases in your flexibility. Likewise, once you stop your stretching program, the flexibility gains will be lost over time. And keep in mind you may also notice inflexibility in other areas of your life. It is all connected.

I think when we can integrate as many different types of creative, effective and energizing movement into our lifestyle, this helps us on so many different levels. It allows us to be flexible, open to the new, stretch our self beyond our self imposed limits, so we never get stuck into a limited routine and become bored or injured from training the same muscle groups over and over, year after year.

Variety of Exercises For Uber Energetic Movement®

Workouts should be fun, creative, effective and energizing! What are ALL the possibilities you can think of for Uber Energetic Movement® that will be holistically creative, effective and energize you? Here are just a few to get you going:

- Running – mix it up: sand runs, treadmil, indoor track, outdoor track, hills, parks, beaches. Go solo and enjoy listening to your tunes, or go with a friend or group – keep it mixed up, fun and interesting.

- Hiking – can be very meditative to connect with nature, can be fun with a group or quality time spent with a friend.

- Walking – indoors on a treadmil and mix up the incline/intensity, walking out doors in a park or on the beach, walking meditation listening to a walking medication CD.

- Roller blade/roller skate – roller away to tunes by yourself or ask a friend to join you.

- Yoga – try a different style of Yoga each week! This could be through a class at your health club or finding a Yoga studio in your area. Another option might be to check out a DVD at your local library and try

out different styles of Yoga and see which ones you
connect with best, then buy the DVD's or join a Yoga
Studio that focuses on the styles of Yoga that you
connect with best.

- Biking – ride outdoors, bike indoors and set the
  stationary bike on an interval training.

- Stairs – outdoors, indoors – set the stair machine on
  interval training, try setting the stair machine on fat
  burning session to keep things mixed up.

- Pilates – many health clubs and gyms offer Pilates
  classes. You might also consider checking out a
  Pilates DVD at your local library or finding a local
  Pilates Studio.

- Dance – a night out with friends dancing, take up
  a community dance course/lessons like salsa, line
  dancing, ballet, jazz to name just a few.

- Body sculpting/static resistance training/strength
  training – in a class, or solo with a trainer or applying
  a mixture of exercises you discovered during your
  reading/research from health/fitness magazines.

- Martial Arts or Tai Chi – sometimes a gym or health
  club will offer these or a local studio. You may find
  your community offers a group class and often the Tai
  Chi classes are held outdoors in a park or on a beach.

- Circuit Training – indoors or outdoors. If outdoors,
  maybe find a park or beach area that has benches to
  use for step ups, lunges, push ups and use any stairs
  or steps – get creative, think play, have fun! You
  could even include using a trampoline for rebounding,

which is really good for the lymphatic system.
Use a jump rope in between your sets of push ups,
crunches, lunges.

- Enjoy your favorite sport or activity – maybe it is
  golf with friends, a game of soccer, windsurfing,
  snow skiing or maybe you enjoy horseback riding or
  gardening. All of these offer creative movement, too.

Rest Days can also be a great time for an Active Day, a day of getting errands done and home improvement projects, gardening, catching up with family and friends – helping them with some of their home improvement projects if you are not working on your own. This IS an Active Day and will allow you the balance of catching up with a friend while helping her with a home improvement project. Remember, it is quality of life and *how* we go about our days and allowing the balance of blending good quality people we enjoy spending time with into our busy day along with those activities we enjoy. Sharing makes life richer, don't you agree?

I have now given you several different Uber Energetic Movement® options. Do you know which options would benefit you best to help you feel and think your Uber Best? Do you think you would prefer to blend the different workout schedules in order to come up with your own unique Uber Energetic Movement® plan? Great! Because those are exactly the tools and guidelines I want to provide you with. You can refer to the Uber Empowerment Lifestyle Plan in the back of the book and write down your Uber Energetic Movement® schedule.

Preventing Injuries

We can only do our best to prevent injuries. By keeping the following causes in mind that can lead to inflammation, this will help you limit injuries – hopefully completely eliminate them.

Are you running or performing the same cardiovascular exercise too many days per week? There is no magic number for everyone to follow; however there are plenty of statistics that show that those who choose to run about 3 days per week have much less injuries. Consider spacing out your runs and the type of cardiovascular exercise, especially at first.

Another way to prevent injuries is to stretch, but stretch at the right time, not the wrong time. After a run or cardiovascular exercise session, is a great time to do some mind to movement stretches and before a run, or cardiovascular exercise session, I would suggest a brisk walk as a warm-up for about five minutes to 10 minutes (about a ¼ to ½ a mile).

A few ways you can take note of any unusual pain or signs of something not feeling quite so right would be:

- Any type of swelling or a feeling of extra fluid in an area like your foot, ankle, calf, knee that is used a lot in running. This is a sign of inflammation. Take a rest day or two or even three until the swelling goes down. Treat with ice and pain reliever such as arnica.

- If you are having loss of control or function in your legs, knees, feet, ankles and as if something is out of alignment or not working properly, rest for a few days and treat it.

There are times when you will feel pain. When you do, I suggest stopping and use this time as a walk break. If the pain is still noticeable when you try to run again, stop the run. This is hard for many to do I know I have pushed through pain plenty of times. This is a time to honor your body and treat your body with respect-enjoy your body, love your body and allow your body to heal. When you practice giving respect, honor and love to every part of your body, you plant seeds of love in your mind, and when they grow, you will love, honor, and respect your body even more.

For anybody serious about breaking out of a plateau or addressing those nagging injuries that keep returning no matter how much treatment, core training is a must. I have a client, Heidi, who is a tri-athlete, who swears by The Bar Method workout. This is also a great strength and flexibility type workout and also great for balance. I highly suggest checking out their site at www.barmethod.com and see if this is the right type of training to add into your workouts.

Knowing When The Shoe Fits

Our feet keep us grounded in life. They hold us up and take us where we want to go in life. They've walked us down many different paths that may have lead to some of life's challenges, but in the end our feet have also guided us to our true path. Our feet also tell us when to rest and even when we may be very resistant to change in life. As I mentioned earlier, if you've ever felt a tightness or chronic pain in your left foot, this may indicate you are holding onto the past and are resistant to changing or accepting and being open to new beliefs. "Letting go" of the old ways that are no longer working for you. If you have felt pain in your right foot or tightness you may be having a hard time with moving forward in your life or may fear stepping into the unknown future. So it is important to listen to subtle signs from even our feet. Even a major ongoing pain that started from no where in your foot could even possibly mean you have pain or infection somewhere else in your body—I had a friend once who had pain all of a sudden in his foot and it was actually an impacted tooth! There are meridians and nerves through out our bodies trying to communicate to us all the time. It is amazing how it is all connected, isn't it?

So how can we care for our feet so they can help us step by step in reaching our Uber Best? One thing we can do is, avoid injuries with proper shoes. This requires a major responsibility on your part. Let's take a look at running shoes.

You will no doubt see and hear many commercials in the media and many advertisements in sport magazines selling their brand to you. Just because it is a well known brand and considered a "marathon training shoe" does not mean this is the right shoe for you. Just as there is a job for every one, and no one job is for everyone, same with the proper fitting shoe. I, personally, learned this the hard way. I have a neutral arch and I fell for the commercial that advertised a "top marathon running shoe", not knowing that this shoe was best for those who have a lower arch. Wish I had known then what I know now.

The best information I have from this experience and in all my research, is to suggest you have a professional assist you. I like to go to specialty running type of stores that have staff who is knowledgeable and can assist you with a technique they use to watch how you walk and from there make the best suggestions on shoes for you. So from there, try on what they suggest and see which shoes feel the best for you. You will need to try on many different pairs, to find the one that feels most comfortable to you. You can eliminate feeling overwhelmed, by selecting two to three different brands. Make a note of when you purchased these and have started to use them in your runs. Running shoes, for example, most will last you between 300-400 miles. If you are a high mileage runner who runs more than 25 miles per week, I suggest investing in several different brands in running shoes, rotate 2 to 3 different pairs of shoes for each run.

Also, a strong indicator you may need new shoes, is – your body will tell you! It can be almost over night sometimes – your knee or both knees will start to hurt, often. Or your whole body will ache and just not feel right. And with it happening all of a sudden, many people will not even think it is time for new running shoes. And so, they try to work through the run – I know I've done this, thinking it was just a "bad week or an off week for me" and that all would return back to feeling right, magically, on its own in just a day or so. (This is not to be confused with a sudden add on of more miles – if you are wearing proper shoes that are not worn out and/or have between 300-400 miles on them, then adding too many miles too soon, can lead to injury). For the reasons mentioned above, it's difficult to give an exact mileage guide. But here are some things you can do: (1) stick your finger into the mid-sole to see if it feels brittle or compressed; (2) place your shoes on a table and check them for imbalances, such as worn areas or tilting to one side or the other; (3) listen to your aches and pains—they often mean it's time for a new pair of shoes.

Finally, it's important to understand that mid-soles usually deteriorate before outer soles. In other words, don't stick with a pair of shoes just because the outer soles seem fine. If the mid-soles are shot, it's time for new shoes and because there are so many variables. Runners who have excellent form often will get more mileage with their shoes, between 700-800 miles per pair.

Please note, that by rotating your running and workout shoes, this does not mean your running shoes will last longer. The rotating is meant to allow your body to feel better and avoid injuries. High-mileage runners will benefit from rotating multiple pairs of shoes. Did you know that by allowing time for the cushioning foam to fully decompress after a run (which can take 24 to 48 hours) will make the shoes last longer. If you do have multiple pairs in rotation, they need not be the same model. Some runners prefer a lighter-weight shoe for shorter, faster workouts and heavier-duty shoes when they are pounding the pavement for longer period.

Whatever your choice is for Uber Energetic Movement®, allow it to be a holistic and creative movement form of exercise, for your health and well-being and allow it to move your soul, cross trains your mind, and stretch you beyond your self imposed limitations.

I have discovered a system that works for me for my nutrition and exercise program and I am happy to share my methods with you through out this book, however as I mentioned earlier, there just is not a one-size-fits all plan. I encourage you to research on your own as well. You may find you want to blend a few of my methods with your own, newly discovered methods. This is wonderful – I want you to feel empowered!

This is your life when it comes to nutrition and exercise and you must create your personalized Uber Energetic Movement® schedule to include in your Uber Empowerment Lifestyle Plan or seek out a professional personal trainer and/or a clinical nutritionist. Listen to your body-never under estimate what it is trying to tell you. Your Intuition can be your most Powerful source, if you allow it to be AND to trust it.

**Please be advised that my experiences and my opinions and the references cited are for information only, and are not intended to diagnose or prescribe. For your specific diagnosis and treatment, consult your doctor or health care provider.

***Note: I encourage everyone to see a doctor before altering their diet, taking a supplement and/or performing athletic, fitness or other strenuous physical activity. It is your responsibility to evaluate the accuracy, completeness and usefulness of any information, instruction, opinion or advice contained in the content.*

CHAPTER 4

A Balanced Uber Empowerment Lifestyle

"Your time is Truly Precious."
- Nancy Hovde

So far, we have discussed empowering our self with intuition, the right mindset elements to apply to daily experiences; we've explored various nutrition plans and Uber Energetic Movement® to help us feel and think our best.

When you practice healthy nutritional choices and empowering, effective and energizing movement that feels the best to you, this allows you to not only feel and think your best, but to look your best as well. Hopefully, you have or are in the process of creating your individual nutrition guidelines and Uber Energetic Movement® preferences, as part of Tier One, for your Uber Empowerment Lifestyle Plan.

We need to remember that life is about feeling our best and thinking our best so we can enjoy a quality life, that allows us to use our passions and gifts, and ultimately living our destiny and becoming the best we can possible be, in all areas of our life. Balancing our life and managing stress can help us achieve a life we truly love. Life IS about balance in all areas of our life.

With out balance in one area, this can lead to feeling unfulfilled in other areas – emotionally and physically and mentally – it is all connected, right? A good day happens when focusing only on those things that give you energy and MORE energy and choosing not to focus on things that drain your energy. Your time is precious. Choosing to live your life, today, with love – self love and self care for yourself and love for others – along with positive and healthy habits and integrating the Ten Element Mindset Approaches into your daily life experiences, can lead you to a life of happiness.

By choosing to intentionally put effort and focus in creating harmony and inner peace into your life, it is amazing how much more balanced your life can be. Time is precious… time never stands still, sometimes we wish it would, like when we are surrounded by people and places we love to be, times when we wish we could freeze the moment, because we are enjoying the connection with the person or the moment we are so strongly in sync with, we wish to make the connection even stronger. Time does not stand still. Enjoy and make the most of every moment. Realize how sacred time is and make a date with yourself – YOU deserve your life. Time is to live it and enjoy it. The Joy is found in the present moment. Simply living your life *fully* in the present can bring you amazing results.

Lifestyle Strategies To Maintain Balance

Some lifestyle strategies I would suggest to maintain balance in your Uber Empowerment Lifestyle Plan are:

- Quality Sleep
- Life Balance to Eliminate Injuries & Illness
- Uber Self Rituals

Uber Empowered Beings Require Quality Sleep

Ah, sleep! Quality sleep is vital to good health. If you want to feel your best and think your best in this lifetime, you will need to get not only enough sleep, but even more importantly, *good quality sleep*. When a person is sleep deprived, this can lead to depression, lack of motivation, injuries, illnesses, poor performance in all areas of their life, as well as leading to hypoglycemia.

Both being sleep deprived and hypoglycemia can cause high carbohydrate cravings. And then, to emotional eating, which can lead to other issues such as being overweight and cardiovascular disease, to name a few. And during deep quality sleep, is when our bodies go through the repair process and prepare us for our next workout and really our life performance.

Keep in mind, to always listen to your body. As Voltaire quotes:

> *"Every man should be his own physician. We ought to assist, and not force nature. Eat with moderation what*

agrees with your constitution. Nothing is good for the body but what we can digest. What medicine can procure digestion? Exercise. What will recruit strength? Sleep. What will alleviate incurable evils? Patience."

If your body is trying to tell you it needs more sleep, find a solution that will allow you *quality* sleep. I mentioned earlier in this book, a resource for you in finding out if you have any vitamin deficiencies or hormonal imbalances, among other hidden causes to feeling sluggish, depressed and fatigued to name just a few. If you are having sleep issues such as not being able to fall asleep or being able to fall asleep but waking in the middle of the night and not being able to go back to sleep, this is something that requires finding out the cause.

I can't stress enough how essential sleep is in restoring health to your mind and body. Research has shown that people who sleep 7 to 8 hours, of quality sleep, each night live longer and healthier lives than those who sleep fewer hours and/or poor quality of sleep. The right amount of sleep will allow you to feel your Uber best and think your Uber best, as well as, better to cope with whatever life situations or challenges may come your way. If you do not receive the right amount of sleep, you have increased risk of suffering from fatigue, weight gain, increased tension and stress. Lack of quality sleep can also lead to poor concentration, poor judgment and poor reflexes.

Here are a few suggestions that may help you to sleep soundly:
- Develop a consistent regular bedtime and wake-up time.

- Avoid caffeine with in 8 to 10 hours of bedtime.

- Alcohol can disturb the quality of your sleep,
  use in moderation or avoid it.

- Avoiding intense physical activity too
  close to bedtime.

- Eliminate stressful and noisy distractions as
  you are trying to fall asleep.

- There are natural remedies that can help you to relax
  at bedtime such as valerian, chamomile tea, aroma
  therapy such as lavender, a warm bath, reading
  something relaxing and soothing, meditating.

Sleep can also be very healing and therapeutic when looking at dreams. Dreams can offer some great insight, if you allow them to. Try asking the Universe or higher power before going to sleep tonight, specifically what you might like to accomplish in your dreams so that you can use the answers and results to solutions in your daily life. This can be amazing information for you, if you want to contact loved ones or needing insight into the future.

I would suggest making sleep a high priority in Tier One on your Uber Empowerment Lifestyle Plan. Try to view sleep as medicine to your body, just as the right foods can bring nourishment to your body and act like medicine to your body, so can good, quality sleep.

Eliminating Injuries & Illness

"Any illness is a direct message to you that tells you how
you have not been loving who you are, cherishing yourself in
order to be who you are. This is the basis of all healing."
- Barbara Brennan

<u>Injuries & Illnesses Are Life's Lessons - And I Should Know</u>

Let's take a look at injuries. All of us will experience, at some point in our lives an illness or injury that will require a time period of healing. This healing period could be a few weeks, a few days, a time that is extended beyond what we are use to and will keep us from enjoying our passion, activity, workout, exercise, whatever that passion is – dance, run, walking, weight training – you name it. Some type of illness or injury is preventing you from participating in it, for now. This can be part of reaching our Uber Empowered Self.

For the first time in my life, this was not only the first time I injured myself and could not do much of anything, physically, for an "out let" without experiencing pain, this was also a time period I went into a dark mood. Yes, me, Little Miss Sunshine – really, according to my mom, another quote from my Baby Book , "by age 4 you became more independent, very affectionate little girl, so sweet and happy all the time." Well, I was not so sweet and happy these days! More like Cranky Pants from being out of my sport, my running. Those of you who have not experienced very many dark moods and dark moments, experiences like this can be somewhat shocking to the mind, body and soul – our whole system. This did not happen right away, when I injured myself. Actually, the first few weeks were healing, rest and reflection in a positive light. My physical body, my mind as well as my soul needed the rest and reflection. As the weeks went on and the stress fracture, on my left foot, was not healing as quickly as I would have liked, although I was seeing results, I was still having thoughts and feelings of: "just how far are those days when I would run again?" and "Would I ever?" to "And even if I did, would I even be able to run as fast as I once did?" The dark days had got me! I have never been one to be in a negative mood for longer than a day or two! I missed running like never before. My outlet! We just have to remember not to abuse our body by over training or burn ourselves out. Balance is needed.

I kept telling myself I have to pull out of this dark mood that feels strange and find how to live my life in balance – my True Ratio. I finally just chose to Accept my situation and from there developed a strong Desire to learn what I needed to learn during this healing time period in my life. My injury experience and learning to appreciate a balance, is what helped lead me to my Uber Empowered Self. I learned how important it is to have a relationship with faith. Being comfortable with the unknown of exactly when something will happen or not happen. Difficulties can lead us to have more faith. During a recovery period from an injury or illnesss, sometimes all we can do is trust that this, too, will pass and we will grow from this experience, we will be Whole once again. Facing illness, death, or any other type of drama or challenge you may have had in your life, can help you become strengthened by the knowledge that a Greater Power watches and waits with you. In the long run, for me, it was the relationship that I allowed my soul to have with faith that mattered.

We all have to find our own, true ratio that leads us to our Uber Empowered Self—our own personal ratio in exercise, training, nutrition, our life interests and activities and lifestyle choices. We have to reach a high enough level to "be there" this is intensity on some days. How much do we push ourselves today to perform? How disciplined do we need to be with ourselves to eat healthy today? With what intensity do we go about our day, where we can feel good during our run and after and through out our day and still have enough creative energy to apply toward a hobby, a career, our family and friends. Perhaps flexibility is your goal for today and taking a look at all the different possibilities how you can be more flexible. By going with in and listening to minimize injuries and illnesses.

All of these tips that have been mentioned, can help however, once you are back into your workout, following an injury or extended illness for the first time and on forward, pay close attention to any type of tightness you may be holding in your body and where – is it in your neck, shoulders, lower back, hips. Find it and ask yourself questions why you may be holding tightness in this area. Stop during this time and stay in the moment of awareness – avoid moving through the nag, the pain. This can be difficult I know and have done this. Use this moment in time to change the way you are moving that is not allowing you to move with lightness and a feeling of effortlessness, a feeling as if you were running on water or a cloud, a sense of gliding along, being in the flow, feeling in harmony with yourself and the world around you. Continue to ask yourself more questions if you are still feeling that out of alignment feeling – are you out here pounding the pavement this morning because you feel so horrible about the dinner and drinks you pigged out on last night? If so, this is just over training your body—the Whole body, mentally, physically, spiritually. If you answered yes to the question, don't be hypocritical on yourself – trust me, we have all been there before. Congratulations for being aware and accepting your actions. It is time to rise to Uber Level. Do you know what an Uber Empowered Individual would do? The Uber Self-Care Method would be to ask yourself how you can best nourish your mind, body and soul today so you don't continue to repeat the same patterns that force you to push through a run or workout when you truly, deep down inside to your core being, know how important it is to rest your muscles because rest also will strengthen your muscles, rest will rejuvenate your spirit and soul, rest will provide your mind with mental clarity. You will become Whole again through rest. It is time for a day off. Give yourself an Uber

Self Prescription for One Day Off. Contact me tomorrow and let me know your status.

Physical Illness

Even when we take the best care of our selves sometimes illness still gets us. It could be a stomach bug, head flu, chest cold, Uber Self is not feeling 100% and definitely not performing at Uber Self level. Now what? Have you ever tried to fight off sickness? Just go about your normal run or workout anyway, your normal day, your job, tend to the kids and sometimes this actually works, especially if the only symptom is a minor cold.

Now I am not suggesting you try this next time you have the common cold or any other illness. I have tried to do this. I have learned that during periods of illness, it is a time to learn, grow, renew and heal. And reflect on which area of your life may be out of balance – is there an issue or choice you need to be totally still and listen for the answer? Why did this illness come upon you? Did you feel symptoms of illness weeks or days before? Or did these symptoms seem to attack you out of no where? It is easy to get caught up in life and become unaware of the thoughts we send out to the universe and thoughts we have maybe we've been a bit unaware we are saying. For example, "I wish I could have more time for reading, gardening, home improvement projects, etc". Or maybe you've said "I wish I had nothing to do". Well, now you got what your thoughts created! That is why you are now here, feeling blah, can't go to work now and worse, you can't even go workout or run because you feel so terribly sick. Here is your time you requested to do whatever you had thought about. Does any of this sound slightly familiar? I am sure we all can relate to these thoughts because we all have felt overwhelmed and overworked in life at times. It is important not to be too critical or too judgmental on your self right now and focus on more motivational techniques to help you feel your Uber best and think your Uber best!

A more positive way would be to rephrase your thoughts such as, you would like to have more time to garden or undertake some home improvement projects. For example, you could say to yourself, "I love my life and everything I do each day, from my work, to time with friends and family, to my workouts and I would love to include a half day on Saturday this week for home improvement. I wonder what the best solution would be for me to allow some time for this in my schedule. How can I balance my time to allow all the things I would like to do?" This is a much more positive approach and will bring clarity to you. Once you've asked yourself this it is time to be patient and be open to the right message or right answer to be shown to you.

Another reason you may have become ill is you may want more sleep! Your body needs rest. I think this is one area many of us would admit to. Listen to your body and if sleep is needed, go to bed an hour early or even half an hour early the next few evenings. Sleep is truly the best medicine you can nourish your mind, body and soul with. Always give in to a quick shut-eye 20 minute nap or turning in a half hour early on certain evenings or sleeping in a half hour on some mornings. This can be your body's method of helping you fight off a flu, cold or assisting you in building your immune health, stamina and endurance for a major event about to happen in your life with work, your personal life, or yet one more race. Listen to your mind, body and soul. It truly does know best. We just need to be still sometimes and slow down long enough to listen.

And of course, over training can lead to illness. We've discussed how over training can lead to an injury. Over training is also stress on your immune system. We need to balance our workouts and our busy schedules in life.

Whatever the reason may be why you did get sick, this window of time can be used therapeutically and allow you to soon perform again at Uber Self Level.

Here are some Therapeutic Methods I have suggested to clients when they are sick:

- **Reflective Thoughts based on Symptoms of Illness**
  – A good example of this would be a fever. A fever can be your body's way of sweating out frustrations, anxiety, things that are "toxic" in your life and not working. This can be seen as a healthy way of dealing with the subconscious feelings. Allow your body to rest and recoup. This time can be a clearing out and cleaning process so you can gain strength to tackle whatever may come your way. A fever is not a bad symptom – this is a sign your body is trying to heal itself, physically and also on other levels by sweating out what is not good for you in your life. Think about it. Your body is smart. It knows what is good for it and will tell you so. Your body also knows what is not good for you and will tell you so. You can recognize the difference in the good and the bad – when something is good for your body, you feel an uplifting feeling, maybe even a warm feeling inside, a happy state of mind. When something is not going to be good for your body, usually a hesitant feeling will come over you or a confused state of mind, sometimes even a sharp gut warning to not partake in something. Sometimes this could be a thought or phrase "stop! You will be playing with fire" or "please don't do this. You know how this will make you feel".

- **Reach out to those who are supportive and positive influences in your life** – Call a friend or family member, talking on the phone is good. This can lift your spirits. Just make sure to contact the right positive people!

- **Read positive e-mails/cards/letters** – go back and read some of your positive e-mails or letters you may have received. I keep a special folder for these and you may already do this. If you don't, I suggest you start to. The inspirational e-mails come in handy during times of illness. You can also keep these and re-send to friends and family who may need them when they are sick. Also, catching up on e-mails during this time to friends and family is a nice alternative to talking on the phone. This therapeutic approach can help lift your mood and help you to recover faster.

- **Rest & Recoup** – Sometimes sleep is the best medicine when ill. Usually, it is for me. I know that sleep helps heal my body and helps me recover faster. And if sleep is what your body is telling you it needs, then sleep. Depending on your illness, if it is the full blown out flu along with a fever, then sleep is the best thing to do along with plenty of fluids.

- **Relaxing Techniques** – Read a good book or re-read a favorite, watch a great movie or an old favorite movie, listen to some uplifting music or music that allows you to relax and actually fall asleep to. The right rhythm in the music can be very relaxing, meditative and soothing that opens up channels of positive thoughts and positive emotions which can lead to faster healing.

Rejuvenating Techniques – Sit in a sauna or take a warm bath and use some aroma therapy such as scented bubble bath (eucalyptus is very rejuvenating and healing). Visit an Acupuncturist or a Chiropractor this keeps the body in alignment and healthy blood flow.

In times of injury or illness, allow this time to be a healing that will eventually take you to a higher level in your strength, knowledge, wisdom. Have faith that you will heal, listen and trust your body, allow yourself deep soul searching.

I do not claim to know all the answers on healing. I have come to know that a Power greater than me is responsible for *my* healing, the ability to heal is within and through out every cell of my body. I have found that for me, a positive attitude and patience has carried me through a faster recovery and that focusing on the learning process of what I can learn from this injury, has provided me with more inner-awareness and strength to approach my life with.

Over Training Symptoms

Feeling your Uber best and thinking your Uber best is the result of your choices in nutrition, Uber Energetic® Movement and balance in your life as well as applying the Ten Elements discussed in chapter one.

I'd like to focus briefly on those dreaded words – "over training" and "burn out". There are various symptoms when we over train and work overtime. The most often complained about symptoms are exhaustion, poor performance, depression and changes in menstrual cycle for women, although research has also shown that in men, hormones can also be affected.

Much of what leads to these symptoms is too much intensity and/or too much volume. For many people, trying to perfect themselves for races/events/competition as well as trying to perfect themselves in all areas of their lives, has mental and chemical issues that intertwine, and create different symptoms and signs, making this more of an over training syndrome issue.

Positive thoughts are important when we look at a Healthy Body Image of ourselves as a healthy self, but it is only part of that. I think once we focus on what joy we can get out of life and contribute to others, then we can let go of any unrealistic ties to our physical perfection we may have. Living our life in balance with healthy lifestyle choices that we can be sane with.

When looking at exercise, Dr. Philip Maffetone breaks down over training symptoms into 3 different stages:

> The first stage of over training may blend with the normal overreaching—a normal part of training where you ride slightly beyond your ability to force your body to adapt and improve. However, a fine line exists between overreaching and over training. If overreaching results in an injury, even a very minor one, or one not clearly defined (that elusive knee discomfort that comes and goes), you may have gone beyond healthy training into over-training.

> In stage two, this stage of over training is more recognized. Classic signs and symptoms include an elevation of the resting and training heart rate, and often aggravation of the symptoms from stage one.

> In stage three, this is a chronic condition with more serious physiological and psychological ramifications. Often, this includes a career-ending physical injury or

other serious chemical or mental problem. In a sense, the body has given up its fight against over training stress.

By staying connected to yourself, every day, noticing where you are holding any tightness in your body, taking each day, one day at a time and going with what feels like the best self care for your body each day, can help limit injuries and hopefully avoid them.

Lifestyle Strategies To Avoid Career Burn Out

I'd like to ad that in your career, the symptoms can be calling in sick when you have woken up and felt very fatigued and have no "real explanation" other than you *know* you've been working long hours. Other symptoms due to over working and burnout might be mild to moderate headaches, irritable, depression, lack of motivation.

- **Set Priorities and Plan**
  For example, my client Joan, knows that her morning cardiovascular workout is important to her and how it makes her feel about herself and how it can assist her perceiving the events that unfold through out her day. She makes sure to get her morning cardiovascular in on most days. It requires prioritizing and planning. And notice, I did say on "most days" and so listen to your body. Get to know when it is too much and a rest day would benefit your muscles, your mind and your soul much better than forcing yourself through a run or workout session that is not including mind to movement and your 100% Uber Self best efforts. Time for Uber Self Rest! Just one day at a time. Taking a day off can benefit you in the long run.

- **Organize Your Day**
  This can help fit and prioritize what is important to you and your life. Delegate what you can. For example, I have a cleaning lady come and clean once every 2 weeks. This allows me more free time to include those things I prioritize and want to include in my day. It also frees up my mind to focus even better on my strengths, work, writing and my health and what I want to achieve in my life.

- **Do Not Over Schedule Your Day**
  For some of you, this is going to really take some thinking! It is not always good to be on the go, go, go. It is good to slow down and just be – to have some alone time, quiet time. This is when answers come to you to questions you may have been asking yourself. Also, by not over scheduling your day, you will manage stress much more positively. You will be able to listen to your body's needs and nourish it with healthy lifestyle choices and have time for those activities and hobbies you enjoy.

- **Let Go of Perfection**
  This one is a challenge for many of my clients. Once they choose to focus more on this, it allowed me to feel very free. Accept where you are today and know you are in the process of becoming your Uber Self and that you are doing the best you can each day.

- **Plan Ahead**
  For example, my client, Lori, knows when she will be traveling, and she finds out about food and what to bring, gyms or areas to run. This helps her to stay on track and keep focused, especially when she is traveling for work related travel. It is important to

put your best face forward and maintain your Uber Empowered Self. This way, you don't have to fall off the wagon so to say, and slip from all the hard work you've done. Remember, eating the right foods and creative movement helps us to feel our best and think our best so we can be our best.

I have a client, Chuck, who finds that talking to co-workers and colleagues about the sport they love and share with them the active things he enjoys, such as running, hiking, weight training can offer some motivation. Sharing our passion for the sport and activities can encourage each other to maintain while away from home and during business trips. Sharing your lifestyle choices often brings added support from others close to you and can also rub off in a positive way onto others who may have been seeking some new guidance for their lifestyle choices.

- **Lastly, it is possible to experience career burn out** if you are finding you are not feeling fulfilled at the end of the day. This can indicate it may be time to explore other career options or taking on a new perspective in your current job. In Tier Two, you will focus on discovering your authentic true core values that will help guide you in living a life you truly love, including your work in the world.

Whether spending time with co-workers, friends or family remember to always be kind to yourself, by surrounding yourself with those who support your highest good.

When we do encounter a stressful event during our day, it is best to work through it at that moment and let go and move forward. One technique I like is what I refer to as the Relax and Let Go Technique. It is simple, easy and effective. I prefer to do this at home, however if you are in your car and in traffic (as I know I often am!) you can still use this technique, however, you'll need to tweak some of the process, as you will see! So, let's say you are at home, as I guide you through the steps of the Relaxation Technique.

Begin with deep breathing and notice any areas you are holding tightness. Contract all muscle groups and hold for five seconds and then release, let go of the tension and negative thoughts and negative feelings. Do this a few times, until you feel calm and centered. It can be difficult to do the whole process when you are driving. For this, the deep breathing will help you find yourself and center yourself. You can also notice any tightness in your body and where that tightness is. As you breathe out, release any tightness you are holding. Then ask yourself the following questions:

- Why you feel tight in this area and what can you do to let go?

- What positive healthy choice can you make right now? Is it more deep breathing?

- Maybe it is just listening to some music that touches your inner depth, to your core and sends your spirit soaring or maybe enjoying a cup of herbal tea?

- Would emotional journaling, calling up a friend to chat or send out an e-mail to a friend help to release some heavy thoughts and uplift your spirit?

- Would a walk, a run, a session at the gym help let off some stress and leave you feeling renewed?

Listen to what your body is trying to tell you and follow that nudge. It is all a part of reaching and maintaining your Uber Self, in this lifetime. Remember, we have today to live for – this moment in time. A chance of a lifetime faces us, today, this minute. A precious gift you have. So how do you want to feel today? What priorities will make you feel good today? How can you nourish yourself today? How can you maintain your Uber Self today?

When faced with a problem, focus on how you will FEEL when the problem is solved; this can help to receive clues, messages and signs to the right solution and correct path to take. Always focus on the most positive resolution instead of on being right.

As we share with others and talk about our lifestyle choices (what we say), and we take action by planning ahead and being consistent with our positive choices (what we do) and continue to think of what it is we truly need each moment and listening (what we think), we will find happiness each day because we are in balance (harmony).

> *"Happiness is when what you think, what you say,*
> *and what you do are in harmony."*
> *- Mahatma Gandhi*

Uber Empowerment Rituals, Results & Rewards

Numerous studies have shown that lifestyle choices are successful when we remember to apply rituals and to recognize the results we see and reward ourselves from the commitment of time and effort we put into our goals. Reward yourself on a weekly basis. It can help keep you focused on your Uber Empowerment Lifestyle Plan. I would suggest this is something for you to consider. When you know you can look forward to a weekly Uber Self Reward, this can help you see results every day. How wonderful is that? Each day you will focus on seeing improvements from monitoring your actions, your discipline, commitment to living a more balanced life, feeling happier. Some days you may notice all of the ten elements working harmoniously in your life and other days it might be more challenging to recognize the improvements. This is when applying rituals can help ground us and keep us focused. And we may need to dig deep, be gentle with ourselves and notice even the most simple, tiny improvement. What type of rituals can you think of that can help you maintain your focus and intention at all times and in all areas of your life?

Rituals show us how we live our daily life. It is the way we greet the morning with a cup of good coffee, tea, mineral water or even a protein shake and reflect on our thoughts, plan our day and remember to include time for personal reflection through out the day and to plan another 10 minutes of self reflection in the evening. A ritual can also be an action of Self Care, the way we go about preparing our meals. Rituals can help to set the tone of the day, the tone of the moment, the tone of a certain task and give it more quality of life and more meaning.

Rituals before a race or an important event can help us maintain our focus and intention at all times. Rituals can provide a spiritual connection to very event, task, and can allow an emotional and mental reaction to help us perform at Uber Best on demand. Practicing rituals over time help us to perform at Uber level, under stressful conditions and when we have a lot of confusion in our lives.

Daily ritual preparing does not need to take a lot of time. It can vary for the type of event you are applying the ritual to. Some may take a few minutes and others may take an hour. It is important that your rituals mean something deep to you and touch your inner chord so your spirit can communicate to you the right message. Making time for reflection and clarity will allow your life to unfold to your most highest good.

The following therapeutic lifestyle strategies may help you to create one or more rituals on a daily basis: Meditation, Writing for Inner Awareness, Music as Therapy and Reading Inspirational Books.

<u>Meditation</u>

- Light incense or candles.

- Take a warm bath—this can be great at the end of a long day to mentally wash the day's negative or mentally draining situations a way. A warm bath can also be very calming the night before a race. It is good for your muscles and will help them relax and will also help your mind relax. Chances are you will also sleep better.

- Taking time to appreciate how those simple things in life, like watching a sunset, can bring contentment and simplicity to life. Recognize that when you are in balance and harmony with all life's situations and those around you, you can trust that everything in life is the way it is meant to be. Reflecting/meditating at sunset can be a very content and yet such a simple thing in life to indulge and enjoy!

- A certain type of music (sometimes a certain type of music for a specific task or specific event is powerful with allowing you to instantly be in the moment with great focus and intent) Listening to the right type of music before a race can help you visualize yourself performing at Uber Self Level with a light and effortless feeling. Listening to the right type of music can also prepare your mind to focus more intently on your project or work at hand.

- A run (with music or in nature and listening to the sounds around you) can help to start your day off on a good note and help you deal more positively with challenging situations that may come up. And before a race a nice warm up of some sprints will get your mind and body prepared and help to ease some of the pre race anxieties.

- A walk can offer a simple indulgence that lifts the spirit, especially outdoors in an abundance of sunshine and fresh air.

- A hike or walk on the beach, in nature and if that is not possible due to weather conditions, a walk on the treadmill (or other form of cardiovascular machine will also do the job) with headphones on and block outer distractions and bring in inner awareness.

Writing For Inner Awareness

As a writer, I write each day. I have a gratitude journal where each day before I go to sleep I think of a minimum of five things to be thankful for. I'm sure you may have heard of a gratitude journal. I write about something I am thankful for—an unusual encounter and pleasant surprise I may have had—running into an old friend, unexpectedly. Or it could be writing down a personal best time in a race. Other days may be a lot more calm and you may just feel like writing down the basics – thankful for your health and your family's health, thankful for the roof over your head. The point is, when you take time to give thanks and appreciation for all the good things in your life, you are once again focusing on all the positive life has to offer and this way, you will attract more happiness and positive moments.

Another writing activity that helps to clear my mind and center myself and keep me guided on my true path, is to just sit down and write out and process my thoughts going through my head. This can be in the morning, in the middle of the day – anytime you are sensing too many things on your mind and feel you are missing out on the quality of your day. I have once actually, while driving, pulled over on a side street and grabbed my notebook and pen and began to write. Silly as it may sound, so many thoughts going through my head from I need to get my carpet cleaned to when was the last time I saw that client, to should I call up my friend Sheila for dinner plans for tonight? This is not being in the moment. I call this scattered thoughts or scattered energy. Even though these thoughts are not negative, they are still pulling me away from enjoying the moment.

When we are in the moment, we are enjoying life. We are aware of all senses around us. I could have just allowed my thoughts to focus more on how I would like my next appointment to go while listening to uplifting tunes on my stereo. Even during a workout or run, our thoughts can wander and we loose focus of the mind and movement going on. Now, I am all one for going for a walk when I have a lot on my mind or a run to clear my head – I'm not saying to not do this. This is a great way to release stress. My point is, to try and be in the moment, more often. It is easy to get out of balance more than it is to stay balanced. But with consistency, practice, patience, doing each thing with mindfulness, and having the ultimate will, you'll find yourself enjoying each moment more often and knowing you are living a quality life.

The above writing suggestion also works when you have to make a choice and are having a difficult time knowing which choice is best. Once you start writing, just let the words flow. Don't worry about spelling and grammar this is for your eyes only. If you are angry at someone or hurt, for example write down whatever it is you feel and wish you could say. You can tear up the paper to shreds when you are done. You will feel better getting things out of you and onto paper and this will also help you have more clarity. It will bring you to inner awareness on what your core needs are and your core beliefs and if you are paying attention to those and making them a priority in your life. This will get you back on track, centered and balanced and keep you on your true path that will lead to your Uber Self.

Music As Therapy

Music is one of my favorite pleasures in life. To me, music is a must. Especially when running and/or working out at the gym. It helps me focus and inspires me when to push a little harder and to pace myself accordingly. It allows me to have positive thoughts. It improves my runs and workouts at the gym and feels more therapeutic and I feel very peaceful after my workout.

Music is also a great therapeutic tool to use through out your day. Choose music to suit your mood. I like tunes while working and prefer Enigma most of the time. Enigma's music allows me to focus and connect my core being to the deepest level. It is great background music for me and allows me to perform at my best and with the highest concentration and inner connection that helps me listen to any intuitive vibes or information I need to know in order, to connect with the right people that day. I can also write with this type of music playing softly in the background.

Did you know that music has been studied and that the findings of these studies showed that music does have a positive effect on power, pain, disability and depression? (Sieddliecki, S.L., Good, M., *Journal of Advanced Nursing* 2006 Jun;54(5):553-562). This is so fascinating to me! We have our own power to silence pain with music (or a disability or even depression). So if you happen to have a bad hip, bad knee or bad back, I would suggest listening to your favorite CD instead of reverting to a pain pill.

My client, Keith, has experienced first hand, that nagging pain that can get anyone down and in a funky mood. There have been more days than Keith would care to remember, when he was feeling some kind of discomfort or stress in his life and did not feel like going to the gym. It only took getting himself to the gym and putting on his music/headphones, that has his favorite tunes downloaded on there, and with in just a few minutes, Keith explains, "it is as if I have been injected with a calming drug." And studies have been done. There is scientific evidence that the right kind of music can uplift you, ease pain and discomfort and set your spirits soaring.

Research shows that music is a great way to decrease pain and calm fears after cancer treatments and even surgery. I believe music can also can help people suffering from chronic pain such as arthritis, migraines, back problems, and other health issues. I like at least a daily dose of music, if not more than once per day. Through all of my research, I have come to believe music will help increase comfort and lift depression. And, even better, music is a low-cost "medicine" with zero side effects – unlike much of those pain relievers. I would suggest taking your pick and whatever it is you like listening to—Enigma or Rush—try putting on your head phones or turning on your stereo, if you are coping with any type of pain problems. Treating your self with more than one kind of self-love care or pampering choice is good for the body as well as the soul. Some of my clients have asked me if there is a "right" kind of music? This is the fun part about it – the answer is, anything you like- relaxing sounds, classic rock, cultural music, whatever sounds good to your mood at the time and will ring the right note to your inner spirit – that, is good for your body, too. We all know that variety in life is good!

"When we take care of our emotional well-being
this can make us feel young, peaceful and happy!!"
- Nancy Hovde

Keep in mind, music is a great motivational tool to use through out life – for work, pleasure, working out and running. It is nice that there is such a variety – to fit every mood! Change your tunes when you are feeling you need a jump start back into your routine or which ever tunes you feel match your mood that day.

Reading Inspirational Books

Which books speak to your soul? Which books or magazines motivate you to take the best care of yourself through nutrition and creative movement? Are there certain books that inspire you to live a balanced life? Do you keep favorite books and turn to them again and again for inspiration? You know, those books you have hi-lighted, underlined and dog eared? Refer to these books as part of a daily time for self-reflection and inspiration. Try to spend 10 to 20 minutes each morning reading something that inspires you or motivates you or allows you to review your core values and 10 to 20 minutes again in the evening, just before bedtime. Inspirational reading can keep you on track, focused and offer personal growth in your life. You might want to refer back to the list of Suggested Readings in Chapter 2. If you commute, you might find that an Audio Book keeps you inspired through out your daily commute.

Meditating, writing for inner awareness, music as therapy and reading for inspiration and planning ahead can be great lifestyle strategies to keep your life in balance and in managing stress. A few other therapeutic methods for keeping your life in balance are:

- **Color Therapy** can be a therapeutic lifestyle strategy, you may want to consider. Metaphysically color therapy is said to be able to change old thought patterns, release past trauma, and even raise consciousness to the point of understanding our soul's path. I like to use color therapy when I do a Meditative Reiki session. All of our chakras have a specific color and as I lay my hands on each chakra, I visualize the vibrant color for that chakra. This can be a very self-healing method.

- **Hobbies and activities** are endless and should be explored and you may want to experience different ones. There is gardening, home improvements, writing, reading, drawing, painting, collecting collectables, traveling just to name a few. Whatever you choose find an interest that you feel passionate about and practically jump out of bed in the morning to do! If you want to raise your vibration make sure you allow time today for something FUN that you totally ENJOY!

- **Simple Pleasures**, such as reflecting at sunset can be a very content and yet such a simple thing in life to indulge and enjoy!

Empower yourself with inspiration – just get quiet and tap into your inner spirit, listen and it will guide you. Feel empowered to trust the loving wisdom of your heart. Take time each day to reflect on how inner peace creates so much fulfillment and happiness and makes life so simple. Attain it!!

Earlier, I mentioned recognizing results and celebrating with rewards. Each day can offer the opportunity to recognize the results you see in your efforts of taking the best care of yourself through nutrition, Uber Energetic Movement® and living a balanced life. I would like you to add Uber Rewards to your Uber Empowerment Lifestyle Plan. Some Uber Rewards my clients have often mentioned they like to look forward to each day or weekly, as a way of celebrating their successful efforts of taking the best care of themselves are:

- Reading a good, book in the evening (or buying a new book)
- Buying a new workout outfit
- Warm bubble bath
- Massage
- Pampering – manicure/pedicure
- Buy a new aroma therapy candle
- Buying new music to listen to during workouts or for pure enjoyment
- Going to see a movie
- Weekend get-away and rejuvenate

What kinds of Uber Self weekly or even daily Uber Rewards can you think of, to give to your self? I would like to you list these on your Uber Empowerment Lifestyle Plan. Uber Rituals and Rewards can be found under Tier Two on your Uber Empowerment Lifestyle Plan. We will be discussing more about Uber Rituals and Rewards in Chapter 5. Making time to celebrate the commitments and effort you've put into reaching your goals, will keep you motivated along the way.

"Dance as though no on is watching you.
Love as though you have never been hurt before.
Sing as though no one can hear you Live
as though heaven is on earth."
- Souza

Through out Tier One, you designed the first part of your Uber Empowerment Lifestyle Plan. You created the Nutrition Plan that includes foods, beverages and vitamins/supplements that allow you to FEEL your best and THINK your best. You also designed your Uber Energetic Movement® Plan that allows you to feel amazing physically, mentally and spiritually when you choose the right exercises for *you.* And finally, you selected Lifestyle Strategies to manage stress and enjoy living a Balanced life.

When you are feeling your best, you can think your best and be your best. I would like to discuss more on the concept of HOW you can enjoy a truly fulfilling life when you recognize your Uber Authentic Self. We will discuss recognizing your Uber Authentic Self in Tier Two.

TIER TWO

Recognizing Your Uber Authentic Self
Leads to True Fulfillment

Now that you are feeling and thinking your Uber best by choosing to live a healthy lifestyle, it is time to develop a strategy to recognize your Uber Authentic Self so you can experience enrichment and a more satisfying life. Tier Two of your Uber Empowerment Lifestyle Plan helps you to discover your Authentic Self so you can recognize WHO you are and what will bring you true fulfillment each and every day, to live your optimal life. Your Tier Two strategy will be based on:

- Eliminating frustrations through simplifying
  and focusing on positive energy to enjoy living
  a quality lifestyle that meets your needs.

- Defining your Uber Authentic Self by recognizing
  your Authentic Values.

- Creating time for Authentic Values and adding new
  Authentic Values.

In Tier Two, you will discover your optimal life and how you can use your greatest natural gifts and strengths each day so you are living a life you truly love. I really feel everyone of us is here to serve the people we are meant to serve, to offer our most natural gifts and greatest strengths to others and live our true life purpose. You can achieve true fulfillment each day by discovering your Uber Authentic Self and your life purpose.

As before, I will walk you through the process of designing Tier Two of your Uber Empowerment Lifestyle Plan and you will see how honoring your Authentic Values and Living your Optimal Life can bring purpose, passion and true fulfillment to your World.

CHAPTER 5

Living Your Optimal Life

"Man has been endowed with reason, with the power to create,
so that he can add to what he's been given."
- Anton Chekhov (1860-1904)
Russian Dramatist and Writer

Have you ever thought your time here on Earth is limited? It is and so don't waste it living someone else's life. Don't get trapped into the "shoulds" society and the media can put upon us which can lead to living with the results of other people's thinking. Everyone has their own opinions, don't allow their opinions to smother your own beliefs, values and most of all that inner voice, your intuition. Your intuition is what keeps you aligned on your true path and by following your true path you will find your life purpose. Once you have found your life purpose begin to live it with passion. This will take a huge amount of courage to follow your passion, your hearts true desires.

Your heart and your intuition somehow already know what you truly want to become. It just requires you to be silent and to listen. This will empower you to always be true to yourself and keep following your dreams. Remember to keep passion and faith as your guide and never stop believing in yourself. Stay inspired by choosing lifestyle choices that fully support you to become your Uber Authentic Self. Take great care in your Whole Self through healthy lifestyle choices in nutrition, creative movement each day, quiet time/solitude and most of all enjoying your work. When we take the best care of our Whole Self we feel our Best Self. This empowers us to follow our intuition and live our life purpose with passion. It is time to discover and become your Uber Authentic Self!

What are the consequences of when we do not live our life purpose? Often that is when we are feeling frustrated and that day to day life is a major struggle. What are the signs and messages that are trying so hard to get our attention and tell us we are not on our life path? Situations such as the break-up of a relationship that was toxic anyway? Or maybe a job layoff from a career that was stressful or frustrating anyway. Perhaps a physical ailment keeps showing up such as headaches and this could be your body's way of trying to tell you that you are not in the right situation, you are not living your life purpose. We all have an inner knowing of when we are not in alignment with our true self and we all have been blessed with a strong inner knowing of when we are in alignment with our true self. We feel this rightness with the World when we seem to be "in the flow of life". Many times this can happen when being fully present with the task at hand or caught up in the present moment. Or feeling uplifted after helping someone who was dealing with what appeared to be a crisis. This feeling of being in the flow of life should be present in our careers as well, showing us confirmation that we are on our true path and living our life purpose.

Our time here on Earth is short and fast. You are here for a reason. Find that purpose and live it with passion. Believe in yourself and the World will, too. Sometimes it can help to hire a lifestyle coach in guiding you to live a life you truly love.

Eliminating Frustrations & Focusing On Positive Energy

Do you find it difficult to find time for those things you would like to do? Would you like to know your true core values, know what type of activities and interests you are most passionate about? Or maybe discover new interests to add to your life? Are you feeling to drained, emotionally, to even imagine making time for fun in your life?

Many times, we are avoiding or tolerating certain situations, tasks and sometimes even people who bring us down, drain our energy and we just focus on getting through the day by putting up with these energy drainers. You may be aware of this and know exactly which things in your life are sucking the energy out of you or you may have no clue which things are draining you, you just know you feel overwhelmed, anxious and out of balance. If you are feeling like this, how can it be fun or even possible to discover your true Uber Authentic Self? You might be asking your self how you can possibly make time for something like that.

I have a few methods for re-gaining control, re-focusing, and maintaining positive energy in your life. As a reminder, in Tier One, you conquered how to FEEL your best and THINK your best, through designing your nutrition plan, creating your Uber Energetic Movement® schedule and choosing life balance strategies for your Uber Empowerment Lifestyle Plan. Through self care, healthy and therapeutic approaches you will be feeling and thinking your best and this is the most important approach to start with.

However, true fulfillment in life happens when you know your Uber Authentic Self. If you lack feeling fulfilled at the end of the day, ask yourself when was the last time you made time to include at least one of your natural gifts, strengths and focused on it passionately. Your true, authentic self is always more interesting, fun and real. Allow your true authentic self to shimmer, shine and sparkle. Abundance and joy seem to flow so easily when focusing on how to help other people through your authentic strengths instead of only focusing on how they might be useful to you. Converging your Uber Authentic Self with your natural gifts and greatest strengths and how you can use them to help others, will allow you to feel true fulfillment each day.

In order to allow more time in your life for fun, positive energy and recognizing your authentic values, the first requirement is, that you learn how to manage those annoyances – situations, tasks, people. Some may be minor enough that you may choose to delete them out of your life or maybe delegate them. Others may require a little more creative thought and coming up with the right solution. Allow mindfulness to guide you in taking a step back to observe reality, accept and embrace all your options.

Imagine how your day would be when you only focus on your BEST strengthens and how you can provide your best strengthens and natural gifts to others. Be aware of how this might inspire you and just how much our energy vibration rises. A good day happens when focusing only on those things that give you energy and MORE energy and not focusing on things that drain your energy. Your time is precious.

Things that can drain our energy are things like clutter-sticky notes posted all over your desk, piles of dishes in the sink, messy closets, household repairs, unfinished projects – you've started and have not picked up where you last left off, in several weeks or months, maybe in years. These are minor issues but they can built up, over time and mentally drain us. This is because we know they need to get done, it is making the time for it that we are avoiding and we keep brushing these items off. Telling our self we will tackle it tomorrow, will only allow more energy to be sucked out of us. We put up with these annoyances for as long as we can. Unfortunately, these are the exact annoyances that keep us from making time to recognize our authentic self and enjoy a quality life. It is easy to fall into the trap of thinking this is just part of life and normal and we all must deal with these annoyances. This is not the case. We must learn to effectively handle these annoyances.

Applying the ten elements we covered in module one can help. It can be a fairly quick process and need not take long. We must first be Aware of these annoyances and Accept them as reality. At this point, I'd like you to take pen and paper and make a list of all the annoyances in your life. List as many as you believe you currently have. You may want to look at all categories in your life such as:

- Career/Work/Professional life
- Relationships
- Financial
- Health/Wellness
- Emotional
- Spirituality
- Community
- Home/Environment

It might be helpful to list your annoyances as Energy Zappers. For example, you could list them such as this:

Energy Zappers in Career in the first column and list all the items that zap your energy. In the next column, write Energy Zappers in Home life and list all the items that zap your energy in your home life. You can see an example of this tool used on the Uber Empowerment Lifestyle Plan Example listed in the appendix section of this book.

You may find you have many energy zappers to list in one area and none in the next category. This is okay. The point is, to get these annoyances down on paper so you can see all the items that are zapping your energy. You are now Aware of all the energy zappers in your life. You need to Accept that they are draining you of precious positive energy.

Once you Accept these annoyances are draining your energy, ask yourself if you are willing to let them go, to manage them once and for all – to delegate what you can, delete what can, share a responsibility if you need to. It can help to create desire for wanting to make a positive change – ask yourself how important living a quality life is to you? Ask yourself if this energy zapper is costing you time, inconvenience or loss of well-being. Is tolerating this energy zapper really worth it? Life can be more fulfilling when making time for more nourishing activities that feed your mind, body and soul. Keep in mind that sacrificing for others and always saying "yes" to requests from others or taking on major tasks and extra work loads in order to experience feeling like a hero is not going to lead you to living a fulfilling and balanced life that allows for your authentic values. Perhaps always saying "yes" to others in your career area has led you to success in your professional life, however, the goal to living a life you truly love is being both successful and feeling fulfillment in life.

Creating a strong enough "why" leads you right to Commit to do something about these annoyances – once and for all. Commit to do something about each annoyance in your life if the time or energy it steals from you is not worth it. This will require you to practice Discipline in sticking with your Commitment to effectively manage these annoyances each time you may encounter them.

Arrange for Success by creating an action plan to do something about all of your annoyances you have listed, look over your list and begin to address the ones you can right away. Circle just three items you can manage with in the next two days. Monitor Your Actions is the next element to apply. You can monitor your actions by holding yourself accountable. This can be done by reviewing your list monthly if you need to or you may find weekly works best for you. Eventually, you may find that once ever 60 days works great for you. Add new items when you need to and be sure to eliminate the items you have eliminated out of your life – once and for all.

Here are a few suggestions on how to manage your Energy Zappers:

- Create a strategy for each annoyance. Don't rely on someone to go through this list for you, eliminate each one yourself. One example, might be to choose a day dedicated to completing annoyances such as cleaning up a closet, the garage, donating items you no longer need. Select a deadline for unfinished projects and write this down on your calendar. Perhaps you would benefit best if you out sourced certain projects or delegate if you can.

- This is one of my favorite – allow some of these annoyances to disappear, naturally. If you have chosen not to have annoyances in your life anymore, they will disappear. This requires no effort on your part. Feel empowered with your intentions of choosing to not have an annoyance in your life anymore. It can help, to consciously choose to set an energy zapper aside, if you're lacking clarity on what type of action to take. Choose to focus on something else. Sometimes by not focusing on the annoyance, it disappears.

- Letting go of perfection can help. Accepting you can't do everything at once and view your expectations in a realistic way. Just by selecting a realistic deadline for one of our unfinished projects can help take the cloud of pressure hanging over your head. This method helps to form a short-term-solution and can help take the frustration out of the situation.

- View the Energy Zapper as a learning opportunity or look for what you can be grateful for. Sometimes, life throws us a curve and we have a sick or injured child or parent who will need our care, a job loss. This is the time to choose to find the life lesson, choose to respond to the situation and how you will respond to the situation instead of reacting. Perhaps during this time you will develop a deeper awareness about yourself and others and your life. Choosing how you would like to respond requires a lot less energy than allowing yourself to react.

Applying Balance and Happiness are the last two elements. In chapter 4, we discussed Uber Empowerment Rituals and Rewards. Uber Empowerment Rituals and Rewards help you to reclaim your energy. Now, I would like you to list all those things you recognize in your life that energize you, things you love to do such as listening to your favorite music, walking on the beach, running in the park, visiting a beautiful garden or museum. You may now be realizing that you have not been making time for these fun, Uber Empowerment Rituals and Rewards in your life.

You can add to this list when you need to. Use this list as a system to check the energy zappers off as you complete them. You will feel empowered as you recognize the energy that was attached to each item, issue, situation, task. Do you think if you were to keep your life simple, you might experience more happiness? In what ways can you keep your life simple? Enter your answers on your Uber Empowerment Lifestyle Plan.

Feel empowered in knowing you always have a choice, YOUR choice. First look at all your options and preferences, then choose what feels right in your heart, not what others think is right, select your action on what is right in your heart, what is right for you.

Begin to focus on releasing all negative energies to receive pure, positive energy and more of the precious time you deserve. The more time you have for Uber Empowerment Rituals and Rewards, those things you love to do that raise your energy level, you will be able to smile when someone asks you "What was the highlight of your day?" Remember to allow some time for FUN each day!

What Needs To Be Released To Create Peace?

Going a little deeper now, what other areas can you think of that need to be cleared of "clutter"? Issues such as toxic relationships that drain you, cause you to have low self-esteem or do not have your highest good in sight. Any lingering negative emotions that are tied to negative past experiences such as feelings of hate, anger or jealousy these all need to be released, let go of and made peace with, in order to allow room for your true Uber Authentic Self.

Letting go of negative emotions and negative situations can be done by first, reflecting on what the lesson or gift is in the situation that was meant just for you, to learn from as part of your journey. It can help to remember that no choice you make in life is ever "wrong" but that you can reflect on what was right about the choices you made, hence, often is the lesson or gift that is needed to be revealed and embraced. Have gratitude for the lesson, forgive and release to create peace in your heart, mind and soul.

Once we let go of old, past experiences of hurt and pain who knows what new experiences are waiting to be discovered? Imagine what secret wisdom can begin to flow through you. Amazing breakthroughs can come through when we choose to make major adjustments in our beliefs.

In applying the Ten Mindset Element Approach, I would like you to go within and become Aware of any relationships, situations and lingering emotions that have been a negative experience for you in the past as well as recent. Write these down. All of them, as many as you can think of. Once you have written all of the negative experiences down that you feel you have not made peace with, ask yourself if you can Accept that this is true and is still a reality in your life, even though you thought you had buried these lingering emotions, thoughts, feelings, you are aware of the fact that there is still not a peaceful feeling inside you.

If you can Accept what is currently real and you really would like to make an improvement in this area of your life, consider if you are Willing to. If you answered yes, create a strong enough Desire, a strong "why":

- What would the benefit be in your life if you were to find the lesson in these past experiences, give gratitude for the lesson, let the lingering negative emotions go and embrace the new experiences that can flow into your life?

- How might this improvement impact other areas of your life?

- How will you feel, if you choose to make this improvement? Write all this down.

Once you've created that strong enough Desire with in you to really want to let go of the lingering negative emotions tied to past experiences, ask yourself if you are Disciplined enough to recall upon these lessons you've learned when you encounter similar future situations. These future situations that may appear to show up repeatedly in your life, may seem like similar experiences and are often "tests" presented to us. Anytime, we've chosen to let go of previous negative emotions and experiences, life will still present us with more opportunities as "tests". This is a gift to you that can allow you to stand in your power, recall on the past experience and choose to respond instead of react in a new positive way. If you find you ARE Disciplined to embrace a new way of responding to life's challenges, you are ready to Commit and Arrange for Success that will help armor you against your old ways of reacting.

I would like you to create an action plan for each of the items you have listed as past negative experiences. Perhaps you need to fully put yourself back into that past situation and replay how you would have LIKED to respond. You may find, you first need to replay the situation as it happened. Pick up on the feelings, emotions that took place within you. Now, reflect on what this life challenge was trying to show you. What was the lesson to be learned from this? Find the lesson and release the lingering negative thoughts, feelings. Recall the benefits you will experience in your life by letting go of these lingering emotions. Does the cost of holding onto these emotions out weight the benefit? By hanging onto these emotions will you continue to experience your energy being drained from you?

You will need to Monitor Your Actions. You might find that if you create five Authentic Rules to live your life by, you can enjoy living a Balanced and Happy life that allows for that peacefulness inside you and transcends and emanates from you. These five rules come in quite handy when life tosses us challenging situations.

For example, I have chosen to live my life by the five following rules:

1. Live a Healthy Lifestyle
2. Live my life with Mindfulness
3. Feel Empowered in all my choices
4. Live with Open Mind & Non-judgment
5. Abide by the Golden Rule
   (do unto others as I would want them to do onto me).

It can be of additional help, to list three or more ways you can integrate your five Authentic Rules in your life. I've included an example on the Uber Empowerment Lifestyle Plan in the appendix section of this book. Create your five Authentic Rules you would like to start integrating into your life, so you can refer to these rules as a way to Monitor Your Actions when life presents you with challenges where you are "tested" to repeat your past reactions, so you can respond from a place of love and create more peace and happiness in your life. This will take practice (Discipline), but when you commit to practice the rules you want to live your life by, you will find balance and happiness. We can only reflect on our actions in the past and learn from them; we can CHOOSE our actions for now and the future.

I would like to point out that some situations will naturally rise anger or some type of negative emotion and that repressing your feelings is not a healthy choice. Choose a constructive way to express your feelings, such as in the exercise mentioned above where you replay the situation and reflect, in order to move forward in life and not remain "stuck".

A client of mine found that when she applied one of her Authentic Rules she wanted to live her life by – her Authentic Rule was to be non-judgmental—this allowed her to apply this rule to situations where she found herself in conversations that were focused on gossiping about others who were not present. This was a true "test" to her and shows up often in her life. Her authentic rule of being non-judgmental includes for her to respond in her new approach. Now when my client finds herself engaged in a gossip conversation, she feels empowered when she says, simply, "I cannot participate in this conversation because one of my authentic rules in life is to be non-judgmental." She has received respect from her friends, family and peers as well as showing her integrity and her true authentic self. Anther way to phrase this situation might be to say "I have chosen to practice non-judgment in my life and I cannot participate in this conversation."

Your five authentic rules should be listed on your Uber Empowerment Lifestyle Plan. If you would like to list more than five, feel free to do so. In my experience, most of my clients find five authentic rules is challenging and rewarding for them; however, they do find when they create a new rule to add to live in their life, this allows personal growth in their life and to continue to live an enriched and truly authentic life at their Uber Empowerment level. When we allow ourselves to grow, there is wisdom that can be found in every single moment.

Reflections Offer Perceptions & Healing

It take great conscious effort to practice non-judgment toward others and in practicing a healthy response when others are judging you. Insight can be achieved when we remind ourselves that another persons judgment of you is just their way of reminding themselves to not act in the behavior they are judging. Judging is always about the person judging – their weakness or their strength. When we can look at others as a mirror to us to reflect back to us what we most need to see clearly in each moment, this offers us a moment of clarity and healing. Clarity happens when we allow our actions to reflect our words and when our words reflect our actions. Sometimes, others will reflect this back to us as a reminder to be who we say we are. Sometimes when we straighten what appears to be crooked in our life, this allows us to become aligned and we begin to see the whole world differently. Non-judgment is key. Remind yourself, when you catch yourself judging others, to ask yourself is this really something you are judging about yourself?

Many of my clients have experienced profound, positive shifts in their lives when they have chosen to accept others frustrating qualities as reflections that are "mirroring" back their own insecurities and negative qualities. This can offer an opportunity to first be aware of and accept the negative quality another person is reflecting back to you and ask yourself if you are willing to make a change either with this quality you also feel you have or perhaps you are willing to change how you react to this quality when it is present in others. Ask yourself how your life could change for the better if you were to make this improvement in yourself? Would you be more patient, understanding and compassionate?

If you find your life would be better for making this change, practice disciplining yourself when you find yourself in a similar situation and commit to an action plan of how you will choose to respond instead of react. Your commitment to your action plan is arranging for success.

Monitor your actions. One way you might monitor your actions is to journal about your progress each time you find yourself in a similar situation. Write down all the ways this was a challenge for you to remain disciplined. Make note of how you choose to commit to your action plan and monitor your actions (your behavior). You can hold yourself accountable by asking yourself the following question, "Did your actions/behavior match your intentions/action plan?"

And if you found yourself falling out of the action steps you created to overcome this challenge, write how you would have liked to handle it and plan to in the future. Let's face it, we are not perfect, and we will slip at times, this takes practice, discipline and commitment. When this happens, this is a time to reflect on what more am I to learn right now about this quality I keep choosing to see in others? What is this quality trying to reflect in me? Perhaps you are subconsciously expecting perfection out of others and when you find yourself repeatedly in relationships with people who are chronically late, for example, your reactions to others behavior can offer a reflection of you. Perhaps this is allowing you a time to consider if you are impatient and you would benefit from being more patient?

Reflections of support can be moments of clarity. These are precious moments when we realize at times we CAN support others needs and that the very need we are supporting in them is a need we have avoided supporting in ourselves. This is another way that others mirror back to us an opportunity to release a negative emotion or a negative experience and show us that it is healthy to go through the process.

For example, my client, Amanda, experienced a job loss and she was down and out, depressed for weeks that left her unable to let go, unable to release by crying or release her feelings through voicing to a friend how she felt "wronged" or angry. It can help in a situation such as this to call a friend and explain you just really need to vent and to not take anything personally but to give you a full five minutes to just go off and say what's on your mind.

Sometimes, we find ourselves offering this tip to friends and we explain to them that we "are sorry about their loss and to please call us if there is anything we can do, even just to listen". We are showing our support to them. Yet, when this situation of a job loss comes upon us, instead of reaching out to a friend to listen and "support" this emotional quality we have going on inside us right now, we choose avoidance, clam up and put on an act that all is well and we are dealing with it. We choose this later option at times because we are afraid a friend might judge us of being weak or that our outburst is not acceptable. Or we may just feel too ashamed or embarrassed to express our emotions to a friend. We might be carrying this feeling of sadness of feeling "wronged" regarding our job loss for a long, long time before fully releasing it. We might have "forgotten" about it and yet several months or years later, we hear of a friend going through a similar loss and we immediately are there for them, offering our support. Our own feelings of feeling "wronged" or sadness can come back full throttle again, allowing us to use this opportunity to release and clear it from us.

Life can be amazing when we choose to, first work on and change our relationship with ourselves, the relationships around us change in the most positive way, the key to happiness and success is in our relationships. You can't really have a GOOD relationship with anyone unless you first have one with yourself, if you want to deeply connect with those important people in your life, first deeply connect with YOURSELF. This can help benefit in personal and business relationships. If you want to create a positive connection with another, form a bridge between you through consistent communication.

To summarize, we covered annoyances such as Energy Zappers, negative experiences and reflections that offer perceptions. It is important to go through the process of clearing out these energy drainers and manage them in our life. When new negative experiences come up, deal with them and utilize any of the tools and exercises above in order to go through the process in a healthy manner.

Arm yourself with the tools to manage energy drainers and make more room in your life for Uber Empowered Rituals and Rewards. You also have learned how to release what needs to be released in order to create peace in your life and choose non-judgment. You have learned how to choose to realize what your judgment of others is saying about you and what their judgments might be saying about you. Viewing others as Mirrors, knowing that others Mirror your strengths AND your weaknesses right back at you, clear as a reflection, they are only reminding you, sometimes with no words even spoken. Reflections can be very revealing.

The true source for finding your Uber Authentic Self is from Love – love for yourself and love for others. In order to get to this higher awareness, one needs to first clear negative thoughts and negative experiences from their life, as well as learn to perceive your judgments of others and others judgments of you in a positive reflection and developing a healthy perception on the many different situations we tend to find ourselves in life. It is always wise to first consider, how else could I respond? Do I understand all the issues surrounding the actions of the person? Sometimes, the best thing to do is re-frame your perspective.

If you want to see more love in your life, first build up the love inside of you. This chapter has provided you with the tools to do this. You can now approach discovering your Uber Authentic Self with an open mind and heart, from a quite and peaceful place inside of yourself. This can help you to have a receptive attitude and offer great insight to recognize your Uber Authentic Self. The oasis inside of you is heavenly, recognize yours and then share it with the World.

CHAPTER 6

Discover Your Uber Authentic Self

"Discover Your Authenticity & You'll Know Your Truth"
- Nancy Hovde

Authentic people are easy to recognize; you can sense when their actions come from their heart and you know they are sincere. Your deepest hopes and preferences can offer insight to your Authenticity. Respect and listen and feel empowered to be that. Just trust your intuition! You have an infinite intelligence within you, follow it, allow it to guide you. Feel empowered to recognize your true Authentic self… life is all about discovering your True Self. Feeling "stuck" might mean you've stopped learning. If you have a strong desire, anything is possible.

Do you feel you have a gift or talent that SO deserves a more prominent place in your life? The World would be a better place if you share it with us. You are so Uber Empowered, you owe it to yourself and to the World to be your true potential and to bring forth your greatest gifts. Follow your heart, passion and faith and KNOW you CAN say good-bye to the old and hello to the new. It can often feel like a bittersweet feeling, when it really IS time so say good-bye to what once was but can no longer be and yet so much is just waiting for YOU to recognize and choose.

Your Past Reveals Clues To Abundance, Fulfillment and Your Preferences

Do you know why you are here? Are you living your life purpose? What is it in YOUR life that brings you a joyful spirit, a peaceful soul and puts love in your heart? Remember that you have your own unique purpose for being in this world, it is in your heart you can find and develop the YOU you are meant to be.

Your entire lifetime has provided clues to your Uber Authentic Self. Which special moments remind you of your true core values and which core values did those special moments enlighten you with? The best way to begin to discover your Authentic self is to start by exploring your lifetime. I suggest going as far back as you can remember. Most of us can remember one or two experiences when we were between the ages of 1-10. Many of our most meaningful childhood experiences happened before we analyzed or thought much about them. Meaningful childhood experiences can provide great insight into our life purpose.

I would like you to take pen and paper and begin to write a few sentences or brief examples of past lifetime experiences that allowed you to feel in the moment, joyful, happy – that you felt, intuitively, you were in alignment with your purpose in the world. You know that feeling I am talking about, the one where you think to yourself: "I love feeling that 'rightness with the World', this feeling reminds me that I AM in the flow of life and on the right path."

Start back to when you were between the ages of 1-10 and think of two or three experiences that allowed you to feel fully alive, in the flow of life. Focus on the type of experiences that were a peak moment for you, that offered you the opportunity to be in a positive, peak experience. Then, list two or three experiences between the ages of 11-20 and then

146

for ages 21-30, and so on until you have listed two or three experiences for each age division, up to your current age. Include what you did, where you were, how you felt and maybe even what the outcome was, depending on the experience. In addition, I'd like you to reflect on the following questions:

- Consider what about each experience was it that allowed you to feel deeply fulfilled?

- What was of quality and value for me in this experience?

This is not an exercise to rush through. Please do not let this overwhelm you. Go at your own pace with this exercise. Most of my clients have found that when they list just two examples per age division, this has provided them with effective feedback and answers. I suggest no more than three per decade. The reason is, as we move through this exercise together, there will be more significant information to give you insight.

An example of when I felt I was living my life purpose, was when I had started research for this book. I came across a company who I felt a magnetic pull to their core values and the thought "this is me" flooded through me. I did not look to see if they were hiring. I chose to send my resume to them and faxed it over to the Human Resource department. The person who sets up the interviews, called me that following Monday. She was very interested and excited and told me I was exactly what they look for and though they were not immediately hiring she wanted me to meet with the Director of Sales in my area in case something opened up in the near future, since they were a growing and thriving company. Again, I experienced a rightness, synchronicity at its finest. I met with the Director of Sales and with in a few weeks something opened up. I worked with this company and this was a major step in what brought me to where I am today. I often rely on this "knowing" feeling when I find myself experiencing doubt. What experiences have you had over the course of your lifetime that you can look back on and call on and rely upon when you need a boost of encouragement that your "sensing" something that is right for you, if even for just right now?

I also experience living my life purpose when I write inspirational quotes and articles. My fingers just dance across my computer keyboard, effortlessly, lightly and I am in the flow, in the moment, everything else is blocked out, outer noise is not even a distraction and I am so focused. Most of all, I sense a deep fulfillment, joy, contentment because I know I am utilizing one of my best strengths and natural gifts to share with the World.

Now, I would like you to go to the opposite extreme and consider any type of situation where you experienced struggle, frustration, hurt, anger. Go back to as far back as you can remember, using the same age decades, listing two or three experiences, if there were any during that time period, even just one negative experience can help shed some insight for this exercise. By looking back at these type of experiences, this will allow you to recognize any authentic values of yours that were being violated or ignored. Many times, we don't seem to recognize our authentic values until something becomes a threat and keeps us from honoring and living these authentic values.

Once you have completed your experiences, I would like you to go through and highlight or underline key words that seem to resonate with you. You may also find there are phrases that really jump out at you, highlight these. Next, write these words and phrases on a clean, new page. Now, take a look – do you notice any pattern or theme? I would like you to write a paragraph, three or four sentences, that states your Uber Authentic Life Purpose. Here is an example of an Authentic Life Purpose Statement:

My Uber Authentic Life Purpose work is to be supportive of self and others to create a personalized lifestyle empowerment plan; by living a healthy and balanced lifestyle through nourishing mind, body and soul; discovering creative and fun pursuits that allow enjoyment and fulfillment each day; sharing quality time connecting through quality conversations together we manifest a life of love and empowerment to be our true, Uber Authentic Self.

Another Example might be:

My Uber Authentic Life Purpose is to embrace knowledge and share wisdom with the world through learning, writing and empowering myself and others.

Again, do not feel overwhelmed by this exercise. Allow your Uber Authentic Life Purpose Statement to brew for a few days. It might be helpful to read it out loud to yourself and get a sense of which words really resonate with you. A true Uber Authentic Life Purpose Statement will:

- Energize you and magnetize you toward it.

- It will give you a strong sense of "knowing" when your purpose rings clarity, similar to that sense of 'rightness with the World', feeling in the 'flow of life'.

- You should feel a strong connection with what you've written and have deep desire to make this a reality in your life.

- Your unique interests effortlessly and naturally pull you toward fulfilling it.

- You feel deeply content when you visualize yourself acting in sync with it.

Be proud of yourself! You have just identified your Uber Authentic Life Purpose Statement, you have taken a huge step forward to manifesting this and creating a life you will truly love and find fulfillment in.

Keep in mind that your Uber Authentic Life Purpose Statement can be lived in almost any moment. Each moment offers you an opportunity to live your life purpose. It is always your choice to find the most fulfilling ways to experience your Uber Authentic Life Purpose, be it in work, hobbies, relationships, and other life experiences, you can consciously choose to live your Uber Authentic Life Purpose.

Exploring and discovering your life purpose work can be very therapeutic and I know this book can help you with that. Deep change is a spiritual process and offers personal growth in many ways. The benefits of knowing your life purpose come when you realize you can use your Uber Authentic Life Purpose Statement as a guide to make choices that lead to an authentic and fulfilling life that you truly love. You may also find that you have more clarity on any new opportunities and new choices that come your way or choices you may need to release.

Additional life purpose coaching can be beneficial as well. Many of my clients have been living out roles that were assigned to them from as long as they can remember by their family, society and the media. They realize these old ways are not working for them anymore and want to find their authentic self so they can live a life that fulfills them, one that is uniquely their own. My clients quite often find their Uber Authentic Self has nothing to do with their past, the images that have been influenced on them from society and the media or their family's plans for them. In order to live your authentic life purpose, knowing your true core values is important.

Your Authentic True Core Values

We have discussed how, sometimes, we "out grow" ways of thinking, old beliefs, old patterns and maybe even certain items of clothes or items you find are no longer useful-they just no longer serve our highest good. Let them go... release them... just let go of them. Make room for the new.

Look inside your heart, look inside your soul and give others your gifts, wisdom, love and kindness. When you choose your strengths and gifts, know that you are also choosing your success. The World needs YOUR gifts; your gifts are brilliant and you are magnificent. All of us have a Being within ourselves to bring to life... allow this to unfold in its own time and at its own pace, have patience; but DO allow it to begin. Taking action involves a journey, begins with one step—recognize and become your True and Authentic Self.

You are empowered to decide how you would like to positively change yourself. How empowered would you feel if you were to walk the path of your own heart? Most of us have three to five deep, authentic true core values that dwell within us. It is very likely they have been with us since childhood. You can trust that these same authentic true core values will continue to be within you for many years. They show up through out your lifetime. It is important to really know your true authentic core values. Your authentic values can inspire you to live a fully enriched life.

Values are beliefs, qualities or philosophies that are meaningful to you, so much so that you are willing to create the life you want through your actions to live these values. When you know your true authentic true core values this can help lead you to make the right choices, take certain actions that will lead you to specific results.

A Value is a belief... a feeling, idea and opinion—about a standard way of life, that is considered to be true and desirable. However, you have your own Authentic True Core Values, whether or not you are consciously aware of them. Through out your lifetime, chances are, you have subconsciously or consciously chosen to apply these various types of values and found some to create joy in your life and some have created confusion or stress.

Unnecessary "Shoulds"

Have you ever recognized times in your life when you've adopted something that was actually quite shallow and did not feel fully authentic to you? These are values you hold that come from things you think you should believe or act in accordance with. These are usually messages you've accepted through the media, from parents, teachers, church, or some type of authority. These usually started when you were quite young and chances are these values were never fully examined, just inherited from outer sources.

Preferred Values

Do you consider yourself as someone who is always punctual? Or maybe you prefer to use appropriate sir names when addressing people? These are values when you see the importance of choosing to fulfill these selected values because they relate to you personally. You've decided that these are important values to fulfill as consistently as possible. For an example, perhaps you believe in being on time for appointments, meetings, dates and events.

Authentic True Core Values

These are the most important three to five authentic core values you hold. You will know when you are not living your authentic core values consistently because you are likely to feel frustrated, unfulfilled, depressed and sometimes even ashamed or embarrassed. If you are out of alignment with your authentic core values, you will not be living a fully enriched life that you truly love.

Your Authentic True Core Values will create energy when you are fulfilling them through action and seeing results. Chances are, when you live your Authentic True Core Values you will experience a life that includes a sense of independence and self-direction and experience less burnout in your life and career. As I mentioned earlier, your true strengths and gifts should be shared with the World, this allows you to share your love, wisdom and knowledge and help make the World a much better place. You will enjoy feeling more inspired, energized and fulfilled. How great is that? Your Authentic True Core Values are those you naturally want to act on. There are a number of exercises and tools I have used with my clients to help them recognize their Authentic True Core Values. Sometimes it can bring a deeper awareness when we choose to experience things as if for the first time and choosing to be a beginner who has loads of enthusiasm for learning something new.

I have eight effective exercises I use with clients to unveil their Authentic True Core Values. You may find you want to complete all seven exercises or just a few of them may offer the clarity you seek in recognizing your

Authentic True Core Self. However, most of my clients have seen the most benefits when they've completed all of the following exercises.

Exercise One - Recognize Your Authentic Preferences

Here are some creative and fun questions that can help you recognize any likes, preferences or thoughts you have and offer some insight into your Uber Authentic Self:

Think as far back as you can remember and consider those times when perhaps there was a musical instrument you felt pulled to. Isn't it interesting how we each seem to connect with a specific musical instrument that strikes a deep chord with in us that makes us want to express our soul?

What is your favorite time of day? What is it about this time of day that you look forward to each day?

Who was your favorite mentor when growing up? And how about now?

Were you one of those kids who always just knew what you wanted to be when growing up? If so, at what age did you know?

Remember when you were a kid and played with the classic metal slinky? And the hula-hoop and going to the Roller Rink rocked?! Depending on your age, maybe it was learning to Roller Blade.

Dreams can offer some great insight, if you allow them to. Try asking the Universe or higher power before going to sleep, specifically what you might like to accomplish in your dreams so that you can use the answers and results to solutions in your daily life. This can be amazing information for you... if you want to contact loved ones or needing insight into the future.

Some of the most lovely moments in life are when we resonate with those "meant to read" words that seem to jump out at us while reading. Has this ever happened to you? What type of books do you seem to be most naturally drawn to? What type of books do you like to read just for fun?

Creativity requires to think big and allow your imagination to manifest your true desires, dreams and goals into a reality even if you still remember a child hood dream you once had over and over; this just might be your life passion. Allow this to guide you in creating what you truly want in your life.

Exercise Two – Recognize Your Authentic Passions

What are some things you know you are passionate about? Many of my clients find these are the things that make their eyes light up and their heart sing. Interests and activities that allow you to feel some of these type of experiences:

- You feel energized and motivated, easily jump out of bed in the morning to pursue this interest

- Loose track of time, fully focused on the task at hand, 100% in the present moment, not the past or the future

- You feel alive, energized and life is good

- You are fearless, any obstacles you might encounter you by pass easily and effortlessly.

Exercise Three – Recognize Your Authentic Calling

Another tool I like to provide my clients with in recognizing their Authentic True Core Values is to go with in and ask yourself is there a job, career, activity or interest you have that if you KNEW you could not fail and money was not an issue, what this would be? This could be a deep feeling you hold about a charity, a strong passion you have always had for a sport, activity or interest. This is a great way to discover a core value that comes straight from your heart. By exploring your no-fail thoughts and ideas you will be able to recognize some of your values and integrate them into your life.

Exercise Four – Recognize Authentic Words & Phrases That Resonate With You

Some of my clients have found the list of words below helpful in discovering their Authentic True Core Values. Which of these words below do you feel pulled to or as if these words resonate with you? Circle 10 or more. Feel free to ad your own! Select those words that are most important to you and you feel guide you in creating a value focused life. You will use the remainder exercises below, that follow this exercise, to help you narrow down your list to three to five Authentic True Core Values.

Discovery	*Being an Expert*	*Joy*
Exploring	*Creating*	*Peace*
Teaching	*Clarifying*	*Truth*
Communicating	*Designing*	*Peace*
Inspiring Others	*Crafting*	*Uniqueness*
Playing Sports	*Intuition*	*Spirituality*
Leading	*Ideas*	*Authenticity*
Entertaining	*Playing*	*Flow*
Guiding	*Decorating*	*Energy*
Nurturing	*Writing*	*Integrity*
Doing	*Innovation*	*Empathy*
Dancing	*Love*	*Compassion*

Exercise Five – Recognize Experiences & Situations When You Were Truly Authentic & In The Flow of Life

I have had clients who tell me the following exercise was one of the most effective tools for them in recognizing their Authentic True Core Values. There are two parts to this exercise.

First, earlier, you completed the exercise of those lifetime experiences that you were living on purpose, in the moment – when we went back to your childhood and went through the age divisions and then created your Authentic Life Purpose Statement. I would like you to now go back and ask yourself for each of those times you listed, what Authentic True Core Value were you displaying? Write a word or two that shows the Authentic True Core Value that you were fulfilling in each example.

Second, make a list of 8 to 10 times in the past 2 to 5 years when you know you were doing your best. These are the times when you felt you were living your authentic, real and true, best self; your true authentic core values. Again, go through each of these examples you listed and write a word or two that shows the Authentic True Core Value you were experiencing at this time.

"Ruminate, Think, Dream, Ponder, Contemplate, Deliberate...
Creatively Express Your Authenticity... And have FUN doing so!"
- Nancy E. Hovde

Exercise Six – Recognize Your Greatest Authentic Qualities

Here is an exercise that looks at qualities you had ever since childhood. List five to ten qualities that were a true part of you up until age 12. All of us have been naturally drawn to certain things ever since we were a child. You have some qualities that are just naturally a part of you such as naturally artistic or thoughtful, of a natural helper to others. Perhaps you have always been drawn to numbers and love math. You may have always enjoyed learning about history and have been a natural explorer, loved things that were new and different. Maybe you have always loved to experiment. Use these qualities to provide clues to you in helping you recognize your authentic values. These qualities may be among your authentic core values.

I suggest going through the above exercise quickly. List the five to ten qualities now. Circle or underline or highlight those qualities that are still part of you life and they come naturally to you.

Exercise Seven – Transform Weaknesses into Strengths

Use your highest level of knowledge and insight to understand how you may transform any weakness into a strength and be a success.

Exercise Eight – Recognize Your Authentic True Core Values Through Others

This last exercise can be fun and offer some clarity. This can especially work well if you are feeling "stuck". If you are feeling "stuck" consider finding New Mirrors to reflect your most Authentic True Core Values you would like to add to your life. Choose three people who know you well and can name your authentic core values. Believe it or not, sometimes your authentic core values are quite obvious to other people than they are to yourself. Your authentic core values have been showing up in your life through the choices you've made, the work you do and the things that you enjoy doing (or the things you put aside when you are not honoring your authentic core values).

Write down what these three people tell you. Remember, this is for clarity, just listen, be non-judgmental with this. Merely consider this as additional feedback regarding your true self.

Knowing your Authentic True Core Values will not only allow you to truly recognize your Uber Authentic Self but can help offer you the most centering force within you to be empowered to change ten times faster and have a much greater impact than if you were to just try and change on the surface. Your Authentic True Core Values reflect your highest, most Uber thoughts. Your True Authentic Core Values are a reflection of your highest self, the highest elements in life that are important to your soul. Your True Authentic Core Values provide amazing potential for your success and happiness in life.

When you live a life that is based on your Authentic True Core Values, you will be living a fulfilled and enriched life. You will experience a sense of well-being, self-respect, and have the highest self-esteem. Clients of mine who had once been living a life that either violated their values or a life that did not allow them to utilize their Authentic True Core Values as often as possible, were confused, frustrated and depressed.

By choosing to consciously work on your Authentic True Core Values, such as reading this book and working through the exercises, is vitally important in order to create your personal and professional life around your values. This involves consciously exploring and clarifying your personal values and distinguishing your personal values from the unnecessary should values and those values society and the media and others try to push on you. Do not confuse other peoples values with your own Authentic True Core Values.

Your Uber Authentic Self and Integrity: Applying A Holistic Approach

Your Authentic True Core Values can shift when circumstances in your life change. Life coaching can help you to explore and accept your unique set of values at any time in your life. The more you consciously choose which values will have a high priority in your life, and want to keep living your life with, the more clarity your life will have and the more fulfilling your life can be. Committing to live your life with your Authentic True Core Values can enhance your life to include integrity, quality and fulfillment.

In order to recognize your Uber Authentic Self, part of this process requires knowing when you are living your life with integrity. It is always good to see people for who they really are, especially yourself. Live your life with integrity according to your Authentic True Core Values and allow your actions to match your intentions. The more you can surround yourself with those who value love, truth and integrity, the more fulfilling and enriched life can be.

It can be helpful, to write your definition of what integrity means to you. For example, my client, Patty, told me her definition of integrity was: "doing what I have promised or have said I would do. When my actions match my words; when my life and actions align with my beliefs, words, and behavior."

I explained to Patty that she can recognize when she is living her Uber Authentic Self when she senses certain physical, emotional, intellectual and spiritual sensations with in herself. And that the opposite sensations can occur when she is not living her Uber Authentic Self. I asked her to describe to me the sensations she felt physically when she was living her Uber Authentic Self. I also asked Patty to share with me what she felt emotionally when living her life Authentically. Then, to tell me what type of thoughts she had when she was living her Authentic Self and lastly, to explain to me how she felt spirituality when she knew she was living her Uber Authentic Self. This is what Patty noticed:

- **Physically:** I seem to have a spring in my step, smile easily and often, experience an inner knowing, there is no tightness but a lighter feeling.

- **Emotionally:** I feel uplifted, energized, peaceful, joyful, fulfilled and in the flow.

- **Intellectually:** things make more sense, thoughts connect me to the right resources at the right time and I experience an inner knowing.

- **Spiritually:** I feel a calmness, a heightened awareness, sometimes I can create and write effortlessly for a long time and it flows from me from a higher source.

Patty and I then explored how she felt when she was not living her Uber Authentic Self and how she could recognize signs/messages by listening with her whole self. This is what Patty described to me:

- **Physically:** I sense a tightness in my stomach, I might sigh more often, I notice I don't breathe as deep.

- **Emotionally:** I feel frustrated, stressed, confused, disappointed and overwhelmed.

- **Intellectually:** I have lack of clarity, thought process takes more energy, hard to focus, bored.

- **Spiritually:** Feels as if a big rock is in my chakras and a lack of flow, disconnected to source.

Experienced a "red flag" inside of you? This "red flag" acts as a warning message when you may be out of alignment of your core values and the situation would not be for your highest good. Intuition is the language of the heart; the alignment of your personal truth.

Something inspiring that seems to happen when listening to the spirit and love with in. Your heart has a way of guiding you in choosing what is right for you. If all your energies and focus are going in the same direction, life just seems to flow a little better and amazing things can happen. Trust your intuition to show you the correct path, the right answers. When "yes" = your core values, this always is 100%.

Put your best authentic self forward today. Nothing is ever truly meaningful unless doing it authentically. It is like living your life unconscious. Being conscious of who you are and your authentic preferences equals a better chance of living a fulfilling life. Listen to the voice of your heart, this is your True Authentic Self.

CHAPTER 7

Prioritizing Your Authentic
True Core Values

*"Whatever we plant in our subconscious mind and nourish
with repetition and emotion will one day become a reality."*
- Earl Nightingale

Life can keep us very busy, so busy we often need to remind ourselves that fulfillment, joy and that meaning you desire is always found in the present moment and through living our Authentic True Core Values. Choose to live your life with Awareness and to live in the moment of NOW. If you are going to be present and in the moment, you might as well be in the moment FULLY.

In the previous chapter you identified three to five of your Authentic True Core Values. Now, let's explore how you are currently living your life around those values. Often, my clients realize this reveals a gap between what their life is currently and what their ideal life is. Aligning your life with your authentic values allows for creativity, fulfillment, and well-being. Live your Uber Authentic True Core Values today.

Reflection and Clarity On Your True Core Values

I suggest to my clients, and I am suggestion to you, for one week to carry a small notebook that has the three to five Authentic True Core Values listed. Through out the week, make a note when ever you have experienced a situation that allowed you to feel fulfilled, completely satisfied. Make a note of this on the value list. At the end of one week, look over your list. How many examples do you have for each of your True Authentic Core Values? I tell my clients to aim for six or more for each Authentic True Core Value.

All too often, I have seen a client who will wait until they go on vacation or until the weekend rolls around to enjoy their values. I coach them how we can align their life with their Authentic True Core Values. The results my clients see is how much more creativity they have in their life as well as how enriched their life is. The benefits my clients have experienced is a sense of overall well-being, balance and fulfillment.

Creating your life to be in alignment with your Authentic True Core Values can enhance success, fulfillment and happiness in your life. Each day offers you opportunities to live your values through your choices and behaviors.

It is one thing to write down your Authentic True Core Values throughout the exercises, it is another to gain clarity on them. In order to gain clarity on your Authentic True Core Values, I suggest to write them down on a small piece of paper and carry this with you through out the day, post a list of your values somewhere where you can see it every day, each morning review the list for a few minutes and each evening before going to sleep review the list again.

Reflecting on your values daily not only will allow you to hold yourself accountable, but will also allow you to feel calm, confident and sure, knowing that you are focusing on what is most important to you. You will experience that simple feeling with in you of love, peace and joy more often when you align your life with your Authentic True Core Values. It is yourself to whom you must first be true. Feel empowered in knowing you have a choice and the choice is yours – yours to choose what is right for you!

Creating new opportunities to live your Authentic True Core Values can be an inspirational way to integrate your values into your life. For example, my client, Victoria discovered through our coaching sessions she wanted to use her natural healing skills more fully in her life. She loved her career as a preschool teacher; changing careers was not an option. She found a Reiki Circle in her local community that met once a week. Victoria was able to fully utilize her natural healing skills through the Reiki Circle in addition she was able to fulfill another Authentic True Core Value she had – learning and education. She became certified as a Reiki Master and she continues to read books on Reiki. What are some new opportunities you might create in your life in order to live your Authentic True Core Values?

Creating Goals That Allow You To Live Your True Core Values

Newness—a new week, a new day, new possibilities and a fresh start! When you have goals lined up this can help motivate you to make the best use of your time. Your goals should inspire you and make you smile. You will find when you begin to integrate your Authentic True Core

Values into you life, achieving your goals energizes you even more, allows life more meaning and you will feel more fulfilled.

Just as your core values are true and authentic, your goals should be, too. If you are aiming at goals that have been passed down to you from society, your family, the media and these goals don't feel like the real, authentic you, then chances are not only will you find you may struggle to achieve them, but that they have nothing to do with your Authentic True Core Values. What kind of life is this? A confusing one, a life that puts you in contrast. When we are in contrast we are living a life with confusion. This can drain our energy and our enthusiasm for life.

The idea is not to create a lot of goals at one time or quantity but to create realistic goals that really mean something to you and offer you quality of life. This is where your Authentic True Core Values come into focus. It isn't how much that gets done in one day, but the quality of work, quality of the task and quality of the project.

Here are some Self-Discovery Questions that will allow you to see where you are in your life and what type of goals you may want to begin to integrate into your life. As you read through these questions, you will want to keep in mind your three to five Authentic True Core Values. When we take some time to ask those questions that allow us to explore and discover answers about where we are in our life and what things we would like to see changed in our life, this type of self-reflection can drive us to create an action plan that will help make our desires become a reality in our life. This may feel like work but it can feel like pleasure as well! Here are some questions to get you started:

- How do you see yourself? Describe yourself in terms of how you see yourself today, right now in your life.

- Name three things of utter importance to you, that starting this week, you would like to add to your life.

- List three things you would like to change in your life, starting this week.

- Where in your life do you get most frustrated, overwhelmed or discouraged?

- Do you think there are specific areas in your life that have "unfinished business" and could use some cleaning up and/or closure and healing?

- Is there an area in your life where you would like to become more competent in and perhaps right now you feel frustrated or disappointed in the lack of competent you have in that area of your life?

- What kinds of things do you do for yourself when you need some voluntary solitude, your alone time?

- What skill of yours do you wish you could use more fully?

- What would others say you do well? What do you bring into their lives?

These type of questions can help you take a look at your present life and offer some insight to a more desirable future. True changes happen when we spend time and resources toward developing our minds and spirits, examining our values and letting go of issues that may be holding us back from being our Uber Best in life.

Since you have read this far, I am guessing you feel you are at a point in your life to make some time for creating energy toward fulfilling your desires, intentions and goals. Perhaps you feel it would be valuable for you to manifest these changes now into your life. You may even find yourself wanting to try new options and look at new possibilities and discover if your current habitual patterns are benefiting you and moving you toward your goals or if they need realigning.

Perhaps you have had someone in your life at one time who greatly impacted your life by supporting you and encouraging you to reach for your dreams. This person may have been a mentor, a coach, a parent, a best friend and this person made you feel empowered to make your dreams your reality. Perhaps this person helped to forward your growth and learning. This person may still be in your life and you can still seek them out for support.

Through reading this book and applying the tools and committing to your Uber Empowerment Lifestyle Plan, you can reach your goals and live your optimal life.

Seeking a Lifestyle Empowerment Coach to work with you to reaffirm and clarify your goals for 30 days, 60 days or 90 days or longer can also be an option for additional support and encouragement.

It is time to discover what big opportunities are out there for your life, both personally or in your professional life, that you are not taking advantage of and begin to utilize them into your life. It is time to unveil any hidden strength or skill you have that you would like to use more of in your life.

We can only think for so long, action is moving from thinking to doing. Let us now begin moving forward! Each of us is unique in creating our goals. Creating your goals does not have to be rigid and boring. Get creative in designing your goals so that you feel inspired when you look at them.

Some of my clients have found they prefer to have their goals created on a spreadsheet on the computer or in a word document and they've made some fun touches such as using different color text for 30 day goals, 60 day goals and 90 day goals. They use a check mark for when they've achieved a goal, they put * by goals that are a higher priority to them.

My client, Lynn, insists on writing down her goals in her own handwriting in her journal. Lynn likes to carry her journal with her through out the day and refer to it as needed for inspiration or reflecting on one of her goals. She likes to use colored markers and calligraphy pens, fun and colored stickers (think colored stars!).

My client Mark prefers creating a story. He is a writer in his career. Mark has written a short 2 page story on the computer. The story is in the future tense as if he has already achieved his goals. He reads this each morning for inspiration and setting his agenda for the day. This helps to center him and set the tone for his day. Mark told me this keeps him focused, inspired and energized. It is easy for him to reflect on his goals in his story if he needs to during the day because it is on his computer and since he is a writer he is on his computer a good portion of the day.

Think of all the ways you can create your goals that will help inspire you and make reflecting and achieving your goals fun. Perhaps you might like to post up some inspiring quotes, photos on a bulletin board near your desk or wall calendar. Maybe desk calendar does it for you, where you can write directly on the desk calendar and make notes next to it.

It might be a Daytime Calendar that really keeps you focused and you find this is fun and inspiring. Perhaps you like something more playful such as creating a collage and using glue, tape, paper, pictures from magazines, inspirational quotes.

The idea is to be your True Authentic Self and enjoy visiting and reflecting this place where your goals are displayed, be it in your journal, a collage you've hung on you wall, your computer or your Daytime book, when you view your goals you get excited and add notes, comments, ideas and maybe even tweak your goal as more opportunities show up in your life and you receive more clarity. Allow your goals to offer you creativity in your life and remind you what is important to you. Ask yourself through out the day, "What can I create today?"

Now that you have completed the Self-Discovery and Exploration Questions above you most likely have thought of a few areas in your life you would like to apply some goals to see improvements in these areas. I would like you to make a list of your short-term goals for the next 60 to 90 days. Then make a list of your long term goals for the next 2 to 5 years.

When you have completed both lists, look them over and reflect on how you can live your Authentic True Core Values as you meet the goals you listed. This will help give you some insight on any changes or tweaks that might need to be made in your plans for achieving the goals you listed. In some cases you may find you need to change the actual goals. Here are some questions and suggestions that will help you create action steps to help you achieve your goals while living your Authentic True Core Values:

- Name the Goal. Write your goal in present tense, as if you've already attained it. Listing your goals only in future tense, is allowing your sub-conscious mind to keep it in the future, when the truth is, you want this goal here and now.

- What actions are you willing to take in order to achieve this goal?

- What are the potential obstacles that could possibly get in the way of your progress towards your goal? What has stopped you from achieving it so far? Were you not able to live out your Authentic True Core Values while trying to achieve this goal in the past?

- What specific actions can you take to overcome these potential obstacles?

- Specifically, what impact will achieving this goal have on your life? What benefits will you gain?

- How will you be different when you accomplish this goal? How might your life be different when you accomplish this goal?

- Is this a goal that you can believe will be a reality in your life? Are there certain costs you need to be aware of and are you willing to pay the price?

Again, comparing your list of goals and your Authentic True Core Values will show you if you are in alignment or if something needs to be tweaked or totally changed.

You have just completed listing both your short-term and long-term goals. We've explored what is important to you in life. We've discussed the "what", the "why" and the "when". Next, I will walk right along with you through the process of "how" we can create action steps and dates for completing your goals. Ready? Let's take the first step.

From the exercises you've completed in this book so far, you are well aware that you already have authentic and unique skills. You have the ambition and creativity to expand your ideas in your own dramatic and authentic style. You may already have the tools and resources you need to achieve your goals. You might need more resources. List the resources you will need to achieve each of your goals. These resources could be any one or more of the following: time, energy, a particular network, friends, money, software of some sort. This is just to give you an idea. What other resources can you think of that you might need to achieve your goals? Go through each goal for this step.

Once you have listed all the resources you might need to complete your goal, it is time to set action steps to help you attain these resources. What action steps can you start taking to attain these resources? Let's give these action steps to attaining these resources a time frame and if possible actual completion dates.

Next, you are ready to set a time frame for completing your goals. You now have the tools and resources you will need. Let's select action steps and completion dates for each goal. You will be setting specific dates for completing but in addition, I would like you to include this important action step as part of your plan for each goal. Each day I would like you to imagine you have already achieved this goal. How will you feel? Visualize how you can feel this way naturally, every day.

When you are successful you will feel yourself improving and prospering in connection with yourself and the World around you. Using a holistic approach to tracking your success helps you see how you are thriving in all areas of your life. You will have more energy instead of feeling as if your energy is being drained from you. There are more creative and authentic ways to measure your goal success than the standard numbers method or the "show me the money".

Acknowledge your goal success based on various aspects such as your flexibility, creative and authentic expression, the number of vacation days you will take this year, the fact you prioritized attending all of your sons little league games this season. These are all examples of personal signs of success that light up your eyes, leave warmth in year heart, and a glow on your face. What actions steps can you take today, big or small, that will keep you moving toward seeing more of what you want in your life?

Adding New Authentic True Core Values Offers Personal Growth

Your goals act as guidance to you in your life. They will reflect to you when they are in true alignment with your Authentic True Core Values – you will feel energized, inspired, delighted and seem to magnetize the resources you need to help you reach your goals. I suggest to my clients to develop a practice of setting time aside each week to reflect on their goals and reconnect with themselves with what is important to them in their life, track their achievements and accomplishments and to change what is not working. Reflection will bring Clarity but often requires a quite mind, take some time to pause today and go with in, this does wonders for your Soul & feels like a special retreat!

Here are a few suggestions for reflecting on your Authentic True Core Values:

Quickly write down a minimum of six ways you can live your Authentic True Core Values daily, weekly, and monthly. List more than six, if you can think of more. This will offer you true guidance of how you are living your life. A true authentic life allows you to thrive where each day of your life you live your core values.

Look over your current week and put a star next to any area or situation where your Authentic True Core Values were being expressed, you were living your value, or you were enjoying a value. Make note of those areas and begin to become more involved in activities or various ways to express this value. For example, perhaps spirituality is one of your Authentic True Core Values. Therefore, you might find you can do the following daily and through out the week:

- Reading something spiritual each morning for 15 minutes.

- Take a walk on the beach or in a park at lunch time and connect with nature.

- Meditate for 20 to 30 minutes each evening.

- Listen to a spiritual or inspirational Audio during your commute.

Now go through your week and put an "X" over those activities that seemed to have drained you, perhaps they seem to be an obstacle to you living your Authentic True Core Values. Can you let them go? Can you delegate these activities? What are all your options?

Remember, it is always your choice in choosing your Authentic True Core Values and the significance they add to your life and to make them more prominent in your daily life. Knowing your Authentic True Core Values will offer you insight as to what you will allow in your life and what you will no longer allow. Reflect on how your values bring you joy and fulfillment and that this is the true reason you have integrated them into your life. Sometimes, we tend to have a value in our life that feels forced in order to avoid pain. Reflecting on the question of "Am I integrating this Authentic True Core Value into my life to avoid pain or does this Authentic True Core Value really offer me a true sense of fulfillment and enjoyment?

For example, one of my clients chooses running as his primary form of exercise. Bob ran track and field in high school and loved the sport. He continued to run nearly every day, through out college and through out his career. Bob had been running for over 30 years, day after day. Bob began to find less and less pleasure in performing this each day, yet he would continue to run every day, out of habit. Bob had claimed to value this as one of his Authentic True Core Values because it helped him avoid gaining weight. After years of running, Bob now is experiencing pain in his lower back, knees and hips and struggles through each run, this has now turned into an Authentic True Core Value that is forced by avoiding pain and not for pure enjoyment. When I pointed this out to my client that he has a choice and he can choose only Authentic True Core Values that offer him pleasure, enjoyment and fulfillment, a light bulb turned on. Do those activities that bring you joy and allow you to be your authentic self.

All of us have a list of values in our life, but the top three to five Authentic True Core Values we hold should not be impelling us forward in order to avoid pain. Circumstances and situations in our life change and often our Authentic True Core Values will, too. This is why I suggest to my clients to take time to reflect on their top values and determine if a change needs to be made. Your personal progress will clarify where your energy and effort is needed in your life.

The example above, also shows how, even though we develop healthy habits in our life, sometimes we need to reflect on those, over time, and see how well they still benefit our life in a positive way that brings enjoyment and fulfillment. Bob, who has ran for years and out of habit, was still relying on this as his main form of exercise. Uber Energetic Movement® – exercise – should not hurt and bring pain, it should be enjoyed and bring some type of fulfillment and enjoyment, among the obvious healthy benefits. My client chose to create new opportunities in his life that allowed him to integrate this Authentic True Core Value of exercise and living a healthy lifestyle. He became open to creating new activities to increase the intensity in his cardiovascular workouts to balance out the intensity that running offered him. He still runs but has balanced his running with other forms of cardiovascular intensity workouts. He now looks forward with excitement to his Uber Energetic Movement® exercises and is relieved he has no more physical pain.

By taking time each week to reflect and reconnect with your goals you will feel when the time is right to add a new value into your life. As mentioned earlier, your circumstances and situations will change, one of your values may be moved up in priority to your top three to five Authentic True Core Values. Perhaps travel may have always been a value to you but it was not on your Authentic True Core Value list (one of your top three to five values). Prioritizing values can change when you find yourself desiring a higher level of awareness or new level of consciousness.

I always encourage my clients to integrate new values into their life. But before they integrate new values, I have them reflect on the values that have really had an impact in their life; how did this value impact the choices they made through out their life? How strongly did this value play in their daily habits? How have these values benefited them?

In order to really, truly integrate a new value into your life, consider what the value means to you, if you had to define it. Just as the word success has a different meaning and definition to every single individual, so will each value a person chooses. I encourage my clients to create their own definition of each new value they want to add into their life. By reflecting on their own definition of the value, this provides them deep insight to how the new value can impact their life in a positive way. For example, ask yourself the following questions:

- How can you live this new value in your life?

- How realistic is this new value in your life right now?

- Does something need to change in order for you to add this new value?

- Can you create a new opportunity to live this new value in your life?

This has helped my clients create specific action steps to integrate the new value into their life.

One of the most insightful ways to realistically ensure you are living your Authentic True Core Values is to create some Positive Habits. When we live with Positive Habits in our life this is reflecting that we really are living our Authentic True Core Values. These are Positive Habits that bring you more fulfillment and joy in your life. What are three Positive Habits that you can integrate into your life in the next month?

My client, Sara, had listed one of her Authentic True Core Values was quality conversations with friends. We reviewed how this value was progressing positively in her life. Quality conversations with friends, to Sara, meant sharing quality conversations in person, over a glass of wine, dinner or a cup of coffee. Sara confided to me that one of her best friends recently asked her if she could stop checking her Blackberry for messages every five minutes. When Sara told me this, I asked her if this was a habit she had? Not just during her quality conversations but through out the day? She thought about it and determined that this habit was also effecting her time with her daughter, at times, by checking her Blackberry too often. Sara chose to begin a new Positive Habit in her life that she would not check her Blackberry during her quality conversations with her friends. However, since she has a teenage daughter, she would not turn off her Blackberry during her time spent with her friends enjoying quality conversation. She selected a special ring sound when it was her daughter calling her. Sara chose to stop checking all messages in the evening after 7:30 P.M. so she could spend quality time with her husband and daughter.

By integrating new Authentic True Core Values into your life you can enjoy an unlimited path that is your choice and allows some flexibility, when situations and circumstances may change, but always keeps you in alignment and allows you to live your Authentic True Core Values in your life each day. Remember you CAN combine your passion and purpose in life! Trust your inner guidance, just ask yourself what you truly want. You can choose NOW to enjoy life by weaving your Authentic True Core Values into your life as often as possible.

You have now learned how to create time for your Authentic True Core Values by creating goals that allow you to live out your values. You have also learned the importance of developing Positive Habits to support you in living your Authentic True Core Values and reflecting on adding new values. This will allow you to enjoy a fulfilling life and realize the depth of change that is possible when you live by your own Authentic True Core Values and avoid using methods such as basic, simple problem solving or trying to make only partial changes that don't seem to truly fit your authentic lifestyle in the short term or the long term.

Aligning your life with your Authentic True Core Values allows for creativity, success and fulfillment and well-being. Knowing your Authentic True Core Values allows you to be aware of your greatest strengths and natural gifts to offer to the World and live your Authentic Life Purpose. Recognize your unique skills, discover your greatest strengths and live your Authentic Life. It is really quite simple, when we live our values, our life is fulfilling and we feel happy, if we are unhappy, either we don't know our true, authentic values or we do, but we are not honoring them. Stand in your authentic truth. Look within yourself to find your authentic self and you will find your Authentic True Core Values. Live your authentic values today!

You've mastered Tier One and Tier Two. You are feeling and thinking your best through living a healthy and balanced lifestyle, you are finding more success and fulfillment in your life through recognizing your Uber Authentic Self and living your Authentic True Core Values. In Tier Three, we will be discussing how to BE your Uber Authentic Self, by choosing empowerment during change in life, creating new beliefs and celebrating your success.

TIER THREE

Become Empowered To BE Your Uber Authentic Self

You have diligently worked your way through Tier One and Tier Two and by now, I think you understand the importance of choosing healthy and positive lifestyle choices, in order to FEEL your best and to THINK your best and how this can help you recognize your Authentic True Core Values. When you choose to live a healthy lifestyle, use your intuition, apply specific mindset elements, and honor your Authentic True Core Values you will enjoy a truly fulfilled life.

Just like anything new in life, there will be situations in life that may raise your doubts and challenge your newly found Authentic True Core Values or interfere with your carefully selected nutrition plan, Uber Empowering Movement® schedule or the balancing lifestyle strategies you've chose. In Tier Three we are going to learn to:

- Embrace Change through trusting your choices that will help you achieve your Authentic Success

- Let go of limited beliefs through mindset adapters and understanding self chatter

183

- Live an Uber Empowering Lifestyle through accountability, celebration and rewards

You are now ready to move forward with your Uber Empowerment Lifestyle Plan, into the unknown, your bold spirit, faith and passion will help you through it all. You can learn to live in a state of well-being, let go of past fears and negative energies, let go of the old, in order to create space for new opportunities. You will learn how to understand that the experiences that have happened to you does not have to define who you choose to become. This is your choice—you have the freedom to choose. The concepts and action steps laid out in the following pages will help to empower you to BE your Uber Authentic Self.

CHAPTER 8

Your Authentic Success & Embracing Change: Transitioning Into Uber Empowerment

"The Spirit with a Vision is a Dream with a Mission"
- Rush

Your chance to BE your authentic self is NOW. When you have chosen to live a healthy lifestyle as your first priority, then your most effective creation and gifts to offer can happen. As we've discussed, when we feel our best, we can think our best, offer our Authentic True Self and greatest strengths; we can then BE who we are and were meant to be.

You have unveiled a new you through creating your healthy lifestyle plan in Tier One and recognizing your Authentic True Core Values in Tier Two. You are now learning to feel empowered to BE the new you. This requires feeling grounded in your new self when presented with new opportunities and the new challenges that come with those new opportunities. You are now *becoming* your Uber Authentic Self. You are transitioning into the new you.

When you choose to live your life with joy and enthusiasm, this will allow you to embrace all of life's adventures. It takes a huge amount of courage to follow your passion, your hearts true desires, but it is worth the challenge, because when we don't live our life purpose, the consequences can make life feel like a major struggle. Believe and act as if what you want has already happened. Feel empowered and success is yours. By choosing love over fear, you can feel Empowered to be Authentic, life is all about BEING your Authentic True Self. When you are grounded in a core of self-knowledge, you radiate and are truly authentic.

You have a wealth of strengths, skills, knowledge and experience; you are fully empowered to become your optimal in life. You've discovered the best nutrition plan and Uber Energetic Movement® exercises that allow you to feel and think your best. You've recognized your Authentic True Core Values that allow you to use your greatest strengths and natural gifts to live a fulfilling life. This, in essence, allows for a successful life. What I would like to share with you, through out Tier Three, is to prepare you as much as possible to stand in your own power through life's challenges and to become empowered to BE your Authentic True Self.

Now that you've read this far and applied the methods you learned in Tiers One and Two, in order to experience true success consistently, it is important to understand how to stand in your power during life's changes. Things in life change – situations, circumstances and relationships just to name a few. A change might be more challenging at times than at other times. You can learn to become empowered to adapt and embrace change.

Guess what else brings change in life? Success. If you want to apply your Authentic True Core Values into your life and maintain living your optimal life, it is important that you learn the following:

- Understand success and what this means to you.

- Learn how to embrace change.

- Trust your choices.

Know that you CAN become empowered to be who you are. Always be yourself. When the focus in life is on your values, vision, preferences, and your optimal potential, you will be a success.

Your Language of Success

Your definition of success is uniquely yours.

Take a few minutes to reflect and answer the following questions regarding success:

- When in your life have you felt success?

- Which of your accomplishments stand out the most to you? What were you feeling when you achieved that goal?

- What has been your most challenging life lesson so far?

- Bittersweet moments are interesting, they offer so much personal growth, awareness, letting go of something in order to move onto the next highest purpose in life, so much to feel in one moment. What are some of your memories, knowledge, experiences with bittersweet moments in life?

- Now, take a look at your answers. Notice any similar emotions, feelings or thoughts you felt about success during these achievements? What is YOUR language of success? Describe what success means to you. It is important to keep in mind that you want to focus on those experiences that YOU wanted to achieve, for yourself or perhaps your team. Not a goal (or someone else value) that was forced on you. True, Authentic Success is when you fulfill YOUR goal, your values.

Once you have completed the questions above, you will want to write Your Language of Success on your Uber Empowerment Lifestyle Plan. Your Language of Success is found under Tier Three on your worksheet.

There are many paths you could choose. You can also choose the path never before taken, YOUR path and create a trail. This requires love, love for yourself and others, courage, faith and believing in yourself and using your Authentic True Core Values. Be empowered to create your path and you will find *your* authentic success.

Can you imagine no limits? Mediocrity is not all that exciting, feel empowered in knowing you can go above and beyond. Dream and think big! If no one else reminded you lately, just remember that YOU are totally worthy and able to meet all of life's challenges. Independence is empowering, decide what feels right to YOU, it is your right to choose. Discover an unlimited life.

Keep focusing on what energizes you and fulfills you, this usually means focusing on your natural gifts and strengths, what your goals are and continue to work on becoming empowered to be your Uber Authentic True Self. You are a valuable contribution, focus on intention, consciousness and love.

When we hold others and our self in high regard and focus on who we've become and not only on what we have accomplished, this is true success. Success can also be achieved in knowing that the more you help and inspire others the more you are helping and inspiring yourself. When we speak words of kindness, success can be felt in our hearts. Whether you express yourself verbally or through your actions or words, communicate through love, truth and with clarity. Allow love to motivate and guide you.

Another day ahead to be filled with love, creativity, fun and success! To your own life be You. Just Be. Be True. And Simple. See what might happen. Follow your heart, don't look back and the Universe will provide you with a nice surprise. Some people only imagine their dreams, feel empowered to begin to live your dreams!

Change Needs to Happen To Allow Success

Do you know what your unique interchange of success is? By this, I am referring to taking inventory of your life and reflecting on your Authentic True Core Values, at what distance are you willing to go? How intense are you willing to push yourself? This is why it is important to understand your own language of success. Don't compromise your life and relationships by trying to achieve rewards and external approval of success, achieve YOUR success.

As we discussed in chapter 7, we can measure our goals by a more holistic measurement of success. But when life brings on new challenges, situations and opportunities, you will need to reflect back on your Authentic Life Purpose, your Authentic True Core Values, and your goals you've created for yourself. Then, factor in how these new opportunities that are being presented to you fit into your authentic life. Consider what you will have to give up in order to be successful at this new opportunity. Perhaps you know you could be successful with this new opportunity, but this new opportunity would create imbalance in many other areas of you life. Knowing what your language of success is to you, can help guide you in choosing when to add a new opportunity or let it pass for now. Your language of success should be in alignment with your Authentic Life Purpose Statement and your Authentic True Core Values. If it is not, then you are most likely experiencing contrast, confusion or struggle in your life.

An opportunity may come up where you feel challenged. Perhaps you have been presented an opportunity, for a reason at this time in your life and you may feel a little unsure of which action to take. Opportunities will always be present. You can make the choice by reflecting on your Authentic True Core Values. If the choice feels right, do it with your full passion. If the opportunity does not feel right at this time, be willing to let it go and know that a better opportunity is coming at a better time, just for you. Continue to have patience.

A path may end or change, perhaps you out grew this path, allow this to be an opportunity for rebirth, renewal and empower yourself that you CAN embrace change. Perhaps this new opportunity will allow you to step out of your comfort zone and explore new territory, stretch yourself and grow both professionally and personally. Be open to what unfolds and accept everything that comes to you as a gift, keep your eyes, heart and mind open and you will see that insight, growth and joy can be found in reflective moments. These reflective moments can offer you the right action to take.

It is not so much the change we fear, often more the anticipation that causes the fear and wondering what will change in our life when we make the change. Even positive changes we might want to make, a new goal, often something has to change in our life for us to succeed our goal. Being aware of what will have to change can empower you to make the right choices and to have the courage to go for what you want.

A person must feel ready to make the change, at least a strong enough desire to want to make a change in their life. Even if there is still some fear, if courage is present this can over come any fear, when you are aware of what the fear is. Also, reflecting on the actual opportunity and if it blends and fits with your Authentic True Core Values. As mentioned earlier, this may be the right opportunity but the timing doesn't feel right within you. The interchange factor comes into play here. Consider if many other areas of your life would become unbalanced if you took on this new opportunity. How much intensity will you need to exert if you take on this new opportunity? Perhaps it may be the right opportunity but your young children need your full attention and energy at this time. Know that an even better opportunity will arise in the future, at a better time. Success is also knowing when to pass up an opportunity and when to seize the opportunity. Again, knowing your Authentic Life Purpose and Authentic True Core Values is what keeps you in alignment with living a fulfilling life.

What it comes down to, is when you do decide this is the right opportunity and it is the right time, in what ways are you willing to adjust to the new changes, new challenges and new details that life introduces us to when we accept a new opportunity? It is not possible to know every single detail that will arise with the new level of success you are about to rise to or the new opportunity you are about to grasp, but being aware of the new celebrations and challenges can help prepare you and keep you feeling empowered.

Using the ten element mindset approach, let's look at this example. My client, Sue had defined her language of success, in one of our coaching sessions, as feeling fulfilled through living her Authentic True Core Values as often as possible. Her Authentic True Core Values were: Quality time with Family, A career that allowed her to help others (Sue was a Wellness Consultant), Speaking, Writing, Learning/education.

Sue received a job offer through a healthcare practitioner she knew in her industry. This new opportunity would consist of many new challenges for Sue and her husband to adjust to. Amazingly, this new opportunity would allow Sue to use nearly all of her Authentic True Core Values. The job consisted of educating patients on nutritional wellness programs through workshops held at community hospitals and clinics. These workshops would allow Sue to create presentations and be the public speaker. Sue would also be able to attend continued educational seminars for herself, to further her educational knowledge in the health and wellness industry. Since she valued learning, this was a nice bonus in the job offer. In addition, this job would allow her to write articles for publication in various different hospital newsletters. However, the downside of this job required extensive travel and many of the workshops were held on weekends. This type of schedule would be putting additional stress on her marriage, creating an imbalance in the family area of her Authentic True Core Values.

Sue was <u>Aware</u> of the impact this new job position could have on her quality time with family value. You will recall that <u>Awareness</u> is the first key in order to use the mind set approach elements effectively. Sue <u>Accepted</u> the fact that now is probably not the best time for her to move forward with this job offer, at this point in her life. The interchange was not balanced—she felt she would be giving more of her self in time and energy and would be depleted of energy to give to her marriage. Sue took some time to reflect on this wonderful, almost perfect job offer. She had the <u>Willingness</u> to look at all the options before making her choice. My client decided that she was <u>Willing</u> to present an idea to the healthcare practitioner who had offered her this position. Sue realized this confirmed her <u>Desire</u> of how much she valued quality time with family, as well as how much she valued her career in helping others through public speaking, writing and educating.

Knowing all of this information, Sue used <u>Self-Love (Discipline)</u> to review her Authentic Life Purpose Statement and Authentic True Core Values and confirm her <u>Commitment</u> to living these values in her life. She found that all of her Authentic True Core Values were still the same and they had not changed and that she wanted to ad in a new value. She chose to ad the value of "Ideas" to her Authentic True Core Values. Sue quickly created an action plan, to <u>Arrange for Success,</u> on how she could integrate using "Ideas" into her life. She knew she could begin using this new value right away by presenting her idea of the job position to the healthcare practitioner. She knew she would need to <u>Monitor her Actions</u> on this because in order to present a new idea, Sue felt at times, she was not as assertive as she would like to be. Sue decided she would create a way for her to use "Ideas" each week as a new value in her life. By honoring her Authentic True Core Values and choosing to add in a new value, this allowed Sue to continue living a life that is in <u>Balance</u>. Living a balanced life is what keeps Sue <u>Happy</u>. Sue felt Uber Empowered for honoring her Authentic True Core Values, integrating a new value and experiencing Authentic Success.

Utilizing the ten element Mindset Approach, this allowed Sue to come up with a creative solution to the opportunity that was presented to her. Sue was able to keep her current job as a Wellness Consultant and enjoy the new position on a part-time basis. The idea Sue presented to the healthcare practitioner was that she would speak at the local community hospitals, in and around her city, one weekend a month and contribute to the newsletters through writing her articles. In addition, she would be able to attend continued educational seminars as part of the job's position. This meant no travel and more quality time spent with her husband. Sue would be able to integrate her new value, "Ideas", into her life each week, if not almost daily because she would have new ideas to write about in the various hospital newsletters.

The healthcare practitioner hired someone full-time to cover the other geographical areas. Sue had created a position for herself. Not all opportunities that will be presented to you will allow you to negotiate or tweak something about the opportunity, but by taking some time to reflect and look at all your options and how one of these options may fit into your life right now allows you to explore adding in a new value. Many times, you may have to pass up an opportunity because it is not the right time. On the other hand, the timing might be right, but not the right opportunity.

Your top priorities always come first, always your decision. If something doesn't feel good to you, be willing to let it go. Right time, right place is your intuition, always trust yourself you are on your right path, at the right time in your life and keep believing, have faith, all will fall into place in its right time.

Keeping Perspective On Life's Lessons & Trusting Your Choices

How many times have you been thankful for that small voice that guides your life? Do you remember a time in your life when you made a choice and you knew you trusted yourself so much that you put all of your focus and energy behind your choice? When you choose to live your Authentic True Core Values in your life, you are trusting your true gifts, your greatest strengths and your ability to succeed. When you live your Authentic True Core Values and fulfill your Authentic Life Purpose, you are successful.

Many people know their life purpose or know that if they made a change in life, they could live a more fulfilling life; yet they are afraid and feel "stuck". Realize, this is not "stuck" but a time in your life that is trying to show you, even if you appear to be wandering aimless, you just need to be patient and allow your spiritual quest for knowledge and wisdom to well up inside you, trust yourself that you are on the right path, allow the flow of opportunities to arrive at the right place, the right time just for you. It takes courage and moving forward with your true choice, in spite of any fear.

Feel empowered in knowing you do have a choice when asking "is this an act of faith I am taking or an act of fear I am taking?" Life can be interesting and wonderful when you listen to your soul and see everything else just seem to fall into place. Too often, we tend to over think things, intuitive living can allow you to feel what is right for YOU. Faith can feel empowering when we release the need to know the details of when/where/how.

Your inner wisdom is always with you, the biggest challenge can be to pause and listen to it, trust it and honor it. What if you tried to consciously stop pushing so hard and begin to flow with life, perhaps this might allow more harmony and create more peace in your life.

There may be roadblocks along the way, allow them to provide feedback to you, observe, keep going and view the roadblocks as tools for your growth. View any obstacles on your paths as personal growth opportunities and keep moving forward even when you don't know the outcome, this can allow your faith to grow. Difficulties and challenges allow us the opportunity to experience courage. You can find your courage within yourself, rely on your inner strength and guidance.

As mentioned in chapter 4, when faced with a problem, focus on how you will FEEL when the problem is solved or when you've reached your goal, this can help to receive clues, messages and signs, to the right solution and correct path to take. Perhaps a problem is just something we wish was something else. When a situation appears to not be going in the direction you had thought it would, allow this to inspire you to be open to possibilities, to embrace change and to trust your choice. Feel empowered to be patient, deliberate and sure of your significance.

Focus on what is right about the choices you've made instead of what is wrong. It is easy to associate success with all the right choices we've made though out our life and just as easy to associate failure with the wrong choices; but never is there a "wrong choice" to be made, just another valuable life lesson to reflect on. So, you made a choice and the situation did not turn out as you had hoped it would, allow this to provide you with valuable feedback and show you what you can learn from this experience and how you might use a new approach next time.

Keep in mind that if the choice you made, a goal you set for yourself, isn't happening fast enough or soon enough, this doesn't mean give up. This is time to show your trust and faith in the Universe for the outcome for your highest good. Being patient isn't so bad when you know you deserve the best and are willing to pass up good for Uber! YOU deserve the best in life. Trust that the right answers will be there as needed. Focus on love, it will put you in a higher flow and draw more and more abundance to you. Allow there to be hope and love in your soul. Consider blending the following:

**Love+Knowledge+Wisdom+Trusting Divine Right Action
=Uber Empowerment**

You have your own answers within you and you are empowered to manifest those inner answers into the life you want. The right answers are always there for you. Take time to go within and HEAR those answers. Have the courage to follow the right answers and remember to focus on how you want to feel when you've reached your goal or solved your problem.

In Tier One we explored listening to your intuition to make healthy lifestyle choices from the type of foods you choose to put into your mouth, to the type of movement you will choose for exercise, to which type of rituals you can integrate into your life to help you live a balanced life. In Tier Two we covered how to recognize your Authentic True Core Values by listening to intuitive nudges that have spoken to you through out your life time. We just discussed, in this chapter, the importance of embracing change and trusting your intuition as the first step in honoring your Authentic Uber Self. Moving forward with the choices you've made and being able to continue to trust your choices you've made, when change and challenges arise in life, is what allows you to BE your Uber Empowered Self.

The time now has come for you to choose what is next. See yourself making choices and following with passion, faith and trust, this builds self esteem. Respect follows… others ask "how did you do that"? It is then, your time to be the teacher to those who ask this...And you can. The answers come to you when you need them.

CHAPTER 9

Uber Empowerment Beliefs

*"If you can tell the Voice of Doubt and the
Voice of Fear to be quiet, I think your True Voice would
like to have an Inspiring Word with you"*
- Nancy Hovde

True success and fulfillment is being your authentic self, always. Through out Tier Three, so far we have been discussing how to maintain being your Authentic Uber Self during life's challenges. As you work your way through a difficulty or challenge, focus on the lessons to be learned. Anything is possible for those who believe in themselves. But what happens when we allow our self chatter to bring out the worst in us? Or we start to slip back into our old limited belief patterns? Reality is, this does happen. The good news is, you can learn to be aware of this and overcome those nasty monsters by using empowering self chatter and by creating new unlimited beliefs in yourself and in your life. This will take a mindfulness approach but you know that I believe in you and your abilities. So, are you ready? As before, I will walk right along with you and inspire you to create your action plan of attack against these creatures.

You can use the Ten Elements Mindset Approach: awareness, acceptance, willingness, desire, commitment, discipline/self-love, arrange for success, monitor your actions, balance and happiness; to integrate with some of the methods through out this chapter for overcoming negative belief patterns.

Even the most simple changes you take, the smallest actions of taking control and using your freedom to choose, can boost your inner strength and empowerment. You can become empowered when you become loyal to your inner most truth, follow your heart, your intuition and truth even when others might abandon your truth.

Uber Empowerment Lingo

Where we are in our life today is a direct result of our self talk, that inner chatter we carry around with us all day. Self chatter is our inner conversations we have going on inside of our head through out the day. If you are not aware of this inner dialog that takes place in all of us, every single day, then you need to become aware of it so you can squelch the negative self chatter and replace it with positive and empowering self talk.

In addition, the language we use on a daily basis with others, be it through writing or communicating verbally, works the same way. We need to be aware of our choice in words. And we do have a choice. Let's look at an example or two.

Let's say that you've been dating some people that have been disrespectful of your time, your feelings and they behave in a careless attitude about the relationship. Instead of constantly saying to yourself or to a friend of yours, "I'm through with dating jerks, mean people who are always late, disrespectful and rude!" you might consider saying, "I choose to spend my time with loving, caring people who are respectful of my time and feelings."

My client, Ginny, came to me to work on her negative attitude. If you were to hear Ginny talking about her morning you would hear something like this, "I'm so furious with myself for being late AGAIN for work. I am always running behind. I am the worse with time management. It takes me forever to pick out an outfit to wear that I don't feel fat in. I need to loose another five pounds to feel good about myself. I can't believe I ate that huge dinner last night. What was I thinking? I know I need to exercise more." This is just the first part of her day. Imagine how the rest of her day goes.

You may be able to relate to this through your own self chatter or through conversations with other people. Many times, this type of conversation goes on inside a person, but often, you may have experienced a friend or an acquaintance talking like this. Stop!

Awareness is key. How often are you hearing negative self talk?

Accept that you are talking in a negative way.

Ask yourself if you are willing to make a change? What is the benefit in your life for you to continue to criticize yourself? Would you allow a stranger to talk like this to you?

If you are willing to make a change, create a strong enough why, Desire. How will you benefit if you begin to talk in a more positive way? How will others around you benefit in a more positive way? How might your life be better if you made a positive change? What is the cost in your life if you do not change your negative inner chatter to more positive inner chatter?

Changing your negative language into Uber Empowered Lingo® will take some discipline but if you really want to make this change and have the Desire and Self-Love/Discipline, you can. You can use Self-Love by putting a limit on the negative words you use. The limit should be zero. It will take practice, but overtime, you will be aware and accept that you ARE once again using negative phrases, words, chatter. Remember your willingness to want to change and the whole desire of why you want to make a change for the better. Maintain your self-discipline/self-love.

Arrange for Success by committing to an action plan. Try carrying around a small notebook for one full day – if you can stand hearing your negative self chatter that long. Each time you are aware of yourself having a negative conversation in your head, stop and write down all that you just said, as much as you can remember. Then, turn that around into Uber Empowerment Lingo.

Monitor Your Actions and progress. Carry this notebook around with you for a week. And keep total of how many times you are aware of your negative inner dialog with yourself. Don't be too hard on yourself. Being aware is key and stopping yourself as soon as you are aware, in mid sentence and rephrasing into a positive and empowering new way of thinking, behaving and being. You will find that there should be a better balance of positive words than negative words. When there is more positive balance in your life, there is more happiness.

You want to use empowering words that help you feel strong, uplifted, positive, inspired and optimistic.

After a lot of practice, I promise you the day will come when you finally smile and laugh at yourself when you catch yourself once again using a negative word or phrase in your inner chatter and choose to use Uber Empowering Lingo.

Creating New & Unlimited Beliefs

Just as our words so can our thoughts be self-defeating or they can be self-motivating, become empowered to choose which thoughts, remember it is the thoughts we choose that gives us the energy.

Letting go of our limited beliefs is not an easy thing to do. We've discussed letting go of values and roles that were handed down to us from society, the media, our family and parents. By recognizing your Authentic True Core Values you have discovered your life purpose and have learned more about what you really value in your life and how you can live a life you truly love. Old, limited beliefs can still creep up. Even when we think we have finally controlled any negative inner chatter, there can be times when limited belief patterns will cling to us and they can cause us to loose our focus.

In my coaching session with my client, Brad, I explained to him that beliefs are a set of generalizations we make about ourselves. Even though these beliefs are not facts we act as if they were. Our beliefs form our perception of reality based on our experiences and how we feel about those experiences.

I told Brad that we create our beliefs based on the results of our experiences. These beliefs have become guidelines by how we behave.

When beliefs have been formed, we live our life by them and we will continue through out our life to find evidence to support our belief. I explained to Brad that we become very good at filtering information and messages and we tend to focus on and accept, as true, any information that is in alignment with our set of beliefs.

For example, Brad believed his path in life was not all that important and always worried that the worse would happen to him. He believed it was too late for him to make any career changes in his life. He had plenty of beliefs about why he could not succeed. Brad would continue to find evidence to support his beliefs such as feeling threatened by others success, always being passed up for a promotion – focusing on the worse that could happen to him. We worked on changing his limited belief patterns through our coaching sessions.

There are various ways to overcome limited thoughts. Studies have shown that brain therapy, over time can allow your attitude, actions and behavior to inspire and empower you in the pursuit of your dreams.

From Jack Canfield's book, *"The Success Principals"*:

> *"Neuro-psychologists who study expectancy theory say our brains become conditioned because we spend our whole lives becoming conditioned. Through a lifetime's worth of events, our brain actually learns what to expect next—whether it actually happens that way or not. And because our brain expects something will happen a certain way, we often achieve exactly what we anticipate."*

This is why it's so important to hold positive expectations in your mind. When you replace your old negative beliefs with more positive ones–

when you begin to believe that what you want is possible-your brain will actually take over the job of accomplishing that possibility for you. Better than that, your brain will actually expect to achieve that outcome."

I told Brad that being aware is key and knowing when we are operating under certain beliefs, expectations and assumptions that are not truly our own beliefs. We tend to operate automatically with the beliefs we were surrounded by early in life. Obviously, it is important to abide by certain guidelines to remain a good citizen and follow the law, however there are numerous beliefs you can integrate into your life and live by and still be obeying the law. One of the methods Brad and I used to create new Uber Empowering Beliefs was to have Brad carry a small notebook with him for three days. Each time he caught himself thinking a negative belief, he would write it down and create a positive affirmation. These were some of the positive affirmations Brad came up with:

Old Belief:	**Positive Affirmation:**
Can't Succeed	All the Reasons I CAN Succeed Are…
Worrying the worst	I expect only the BEST to happen

By focusing on the opposite of Brad's negative belief he was able to support his new belief and let go of his old beliefs. Those thoughts we carry around in our head can either help us or hurt us. Focus on your strengths, your Authentic True Core Values, think positive thoughts, you will become what you think. Speaking with certainty allows your desired intentions to become a reality. Using "when" instead of "if" is just one example, notice for a day or two, how you are phrasing your words, your intentions, your thoughts. Your self-esteem loves to hear "I Am" statements: "I Am successful". "I Am happy". Avoid thinking "I can't" or "I won't". "I Am" statements are stronger and manifest in your life faster than "I Wish" or "I Want" statements. Remove the thought: "I can't do this because…" Instead, ask yourself "What if I COULD do this…". Imagine yourself living your dream… NOW. Create all that you see in your head.

If you are feeling despair, know that despair can rob us of all hope, when there is no hope, there is no light and the soul gives up. Listen to your inner guide, the right path will reveal itself. Choose to live without despair, we are what we think; allow your positive thoughts to override any despair.

Being aware of any hidden fears you have about living your optimal life can bring awareness, embrace those fears long enough to understand their cause, then squelch those fears and choose empowerment to go for what you truly want. We can choose to remember past failures or past success, it is always our choice. Do you want to continue to think in limited ways or in unlimited ways. Your choice.

Another method to create new positive beliefs is to listen to subliminal brain wave therapy. This allows your mind to relax into a heightened state of receptivity. Messages are then effortlessly absorbed by the sub-conscious mind and new self-empowering beliefs are firmly imprinted in the unconscious. This takes practice. Listening to brain wave therapy CD's allows you to see a remarkable change in your attitude. Clinically proven technology creates new neural networks that change your brain and allow it to operate with greater efficiency and functionality. Brain wave therapy is based on biofeedback research.

It can be helpful to remember that, sometimes things are not always what they appear to be, looking beyond what may appear at the present, look for the more long term picture. We can accept the way things are, for right now; remembering that nothing is permanent. Allow mindfulness to guide you in taking a step back to observe reality, accept and embrace all your options. We can view these limited belief patterns as only illusions and keep moving forward with positive thoughts and allow the answers within us to spring forward.

You can feel empowered when you take some time to reflect on any hidden or unconscious expectations that tend to influence your actions and behavior. Limited beliefs will only keep holding you back from what you desire. Being more aware of these unconscious expectations and limited beliefs and choosing to let go of them, frees you to create more conscious and unlimited beliefs that positively influence your behavior.

If you can believe without tangible proof that something is so, then you have faith. Feel empowered in your faith, know that you CAN do anything and BE anything. You deserve all you believe you are capable of achieving, even if you don't have the tangible proof, right now. Besides, YOUR faith is stronger than anything.

Feel empowered to have the courage, be who you are and hold unto your authentic beliefs, even when your friends, family and society choose to have other beliefs. Know you are empowered and hold the courage to change these old beliefs that no longer fit the new you. Going through this process, allows you to become your Uber Empowered Self.

Mind Set Adapters to Your Rescue

You want to make the right changes in your life. You have now set new goals for yourself. You have your Uber Empowerment Lifestyle Plan and have even set specific steps and yet – ? No results. Zero. Day after day. You are becoming discouraged and frustrated. Maybe you are feeling stuck or lack of motivation or scared? These are all normal feelings whenever we've decided to make a change in our life. Change CAN be scary. We like being in our comfort zone. We will be talking soon about Accountability in Chapter 10. But before we discuss Accountability, you must have the right mindset. The right mindset for not only just wanting to make changes in your life but also for being able to sustain life'schallenges during your journey and having an effective plan of action. In addition to using the Ten Mindset Elements you've been using through out this book, there will be situations when you will need to rely on some quick, effective Mindset Adapters.

Here are some Mindset Adapters, based on what we've covered through out this chapter, that can help you focus and achieve your goals:

- Change any excuses that come up into a Strong Why. Create a strong enough reason, a strong why you want to achieve your goal. For example, you've decided to start your own business. Each day, you wake up and you have yet another reason that distracts you from working on your business plan. You know what you need to be doing, you've even written down your steps for each day. This is the time to remind yourself your strong why you want your goal. Focus on your core values and this will most likely influence and match your strong why.

- Replace Self-Discipline to Self-Love. Yes, it does require determination to reach a goal. But when you look at Self-Discipline in a new light of Self-Love, it can become your true motivator. Self-Love such as reminding yourself you are worth reaching your goal and deserve to be successful with owning your own business. And so to focus on your business plan is actually communicating to yourself, you deserve success – this is an action of Self-Love and can be used instead of Self-Discipline. When all of your energies are going in the right direction, great things can happen!

- Replace any negative words and phrases with positive words and phrases. For example, stop telling yourself "I'll never finish this project in time". That is a real downer! Focus instead on "I have worked on challenging projects before and I know I can complete this project, on time, one step at a time". This will help calm you, regain your focus on the task at hand. You will feel more confident, too.

- You could even choose the right type of music to listen to while you work and it may help you refocus and boost your mood. Believe and act as if what you want to happen has already happened.

- Replace Doubt and Fear with Trust and Believe. For example, remember back to a time when you made a big decision and you were successful with it. Remember how you felt and draw on that positive feeling, the positive thoughts that helped you achieve that goal at the time. Recall how you just kept focus on your goal because even though you did not know the exact outcome, you just had a "knowing" and kept trusting that all would be well – because you kept believing in yourself.

- Instead of focusing on all the details, focus on how you want to FEEL when you've reached your goal and keep believing in yourself. Your heart reveals your Authentic True Self and the signs show themselves in strong, powerful ways. Trust and believe in yourself and the universe that the right opportunity will be

there at the right time. To force is to doubt yourself,
never force, have patience, trust and always believe
in yourself.

Be open, release the need to control and trust your Wisdom for your true plan to unfold. Remember that YOU are empowered and hold the power within to move mountains. So, by all means, keep going for that goal you've set for yourself, make the change you've decided you want to make; go for what you want. Feel Empowered to take a risk! And remember to believe it and you will see it in your life.

The unknown requires your faith and trust and most of all believing in yourself. We can feel most empowered when we surround ourselves with those we connect well with, we tend to be like those we are most around and our environment/community can often be stronger than we are. You can feel empowered to release old ways of thinking, old patterns that are no longer working in your life and make room for all the new opportunities that await you. Be open, release the need to control and trust YOUR wisdom of your true plan to unfold.

True changes happen when we spend time and resources developing our minds and spirits, examining our core values and letting go of issues that may be holding us back from being our Uber best in life. You have your own incomparable achievements you are Uber empowered.

You can give yourself permission to be and do what you want, keep believing your path is important and keep telling yourself all the reasons why you CAN succeed. Expect only the BEST to happen. Believe it and you've just achieved it. You CAN be Uber Empowered. Through out your day, empower yourself by believing in yourself and your abilities. What you believe you will manifest.

Believe in yourself, believe in others, believe in the extraordinary, believe in the Universe, believe in the impossible. Success is yours. Honor your vision, have courage and keep believing in yourself. Allow your Authentic Beliefs to create wonderful things for you! Know that you ARE of value, never under estimate your knowledge, skills and wisdom to share with others.

Just so you know... I believe in YOU!

CHAPTER 10

Really & Truly Living Your Uber Empowerment Lifestyle

"Arranging for Success is Creating a Solution &
Empowering Yourself through Accountability"
- Nancy Hovde

True willingness is all about you. It is a personal choice to make a change or improvement in your life. Use your Courageous Behavior toward self-improvement every day! Arm yourself in knowing that you are empowered to choose how YOU would most like to positively improve your life and experience amazing transformation.

If taking action feels overwhelming to you, remember that the journey to reach your goals begins with one step... one step at a time, but DO get moving toward your goal and not further away from it. It takes action to be fully living your life purpose, no action is an observer and waiting. It takes just a single step to start the action.

Have you ever wondered why you can't seem to make a change you need to make? Sometimes people feel "stuck" and find it difficult to take action. Fear is usually at the root of inaction. What are you afraid of? Become aware of what it is; choose empowerment to address the fear and continue moving forward with your dreams.

Notice how when you view success as something you do for YOU there seems to be less fear and more creativity, energy and more gratitude in your achievements. Remember, you can draw upon that FEELING you experienced in the past when you overcame a challenge or achieved a goal.

One of the best ways to support yourself in feeling empowered to BE your Uber Authentic Self is to work with a strong solution focused coach. A lifestyle coach can help work with you and overcome resistance to change. A good coach understands using a solid framework for the journey that offers exploring and support for your purpose and desired outcome. In addition, a good coach will hold you accountable to your commitments, goals and action plan by inspiring you to Behave Courageously. There are other options as well that you may use to hold yourself accountable to achieving your Uber Empowerment Lifestyle Plan.

NOW is the time to focus on your gifts and strengths and BE your Authentic Self. Starting today, it is time for you to feel Empowered and to lead.

Accountability is Empowering

One can choose their Authentic True Path in life and develop the knowledge, experience and even the skill, but willingness with an action plan and accountability determines if one truly succeeds with their intentions, goals and dreams on their path.

You deserve the best in life and to feel and be Uber Empowered. Together, we can take steps towards achieving your vision. I truly believe that dreams will come true if we have the passion, faith and we work for them while holding ourselves accountable.

What is accountability? Accountability is a traditional, old fashioned method that says you are answerable for your actions. It is the responsibility of your actions and decisions including the implementation with in the scope of your role or job description (from a career stand point), it is the obligation to report, explaining and be answerable for resulting consequences.

Now, let's take a look at what is considered Unaccountable? An unaccountable person is someone you can easily recognize because they use blaming others, excuses, procrastinate, act confused or ignorant when confronted about why something did not get done, they do the bare minimum required. They will use phrases and words such as "How should I know, it is not MY job". Or "I was never told I had to". And "I did not know". Unaccountable people are slow to act.

Do you already know if you are an Accountable or an Unaccountable Person? In addition to the above descriptions here are a few other ways you can rate yourself. Instead of answering just "yes" or "no", give yourself a rating between 1-10 (1 meaning "never" and 10 meaning "always"):

- I am responsible for my own problems and circumstances.

- I communicate consistently and with clarity with friends, family and co-workers.

- When I make a mistake, I admit it.

- I consider myself a Proactive Person because I often will take the initiative.

- I am assertive and ask if I need something, such as if I need something in order to get my job done.

- I review my daily activities and how I am spending my time and ask "How are these activities contributing to my goals and Authentic True Core Values?"

- I model accountability to my friends, family and co-workers.

- I am comfortable with feedback and welcome it.

It is preferable to have a higher score than a lower score. Review the items and for those items you listed lower scores, ask yourself what you can do to Act Courageously, be Accountable? Write these answers down onto your Uber Empowerment Lifestyle Plan.

Sometimes, you may have the best of intentions yet still do not do what needs to be done, to get to where you want to be. This may be because you procrastinated, took fewer action steps. When you have either someone to hold you accountable for your goals or you choose to use a method of progress to hold yourself accountable in achieving your intentions you will find that the benefits are:

- More clarity, focused

- Less Procrastination

- Fewer Stops

- Achievement of results you only dreamed could be possible

- More balanced and fulfilling life

- More satisfying relationships

A new you, a new beginning will require initiative, action planning and accountability. Are you living your life as a human DOING or a human BEING? Focus on progress by continuing to move forward, allow mistakes to provide feedback, always keep going forward. Focus on how you want to feel when you've become your True Self, met you goal and living your optimal life. What does being a Leader to you mean? Did you know that most high achievers and great leaders in this world include accountability as part of their success plan?

Being accountable is one of the fastest ways to earn respect and trust and feel empowered in your life. When you choose to respond to a method of accountability this gives you control of your life and the power to change things in your life.

After several months or years, some of my clients reach the point in our coaching relationship where they now just need someone to be accountable to. I offer a special coaching accountability package that includes the choice of weekly or monthly accountability, through a series of questions that are related to the clients individual goals. Here are a few general questions you can use to check in weekly with yourself and see your progress or have a friend hold you accountable for your goals and ask you these questions weekly:

- Name one of your natural gifts you used this week and explain what makes that something you appreciate so much about yourself.

- Name one new Authentic True Core Value you would like to integrate into your life and explain what would make that valuable to you.

- What is one action step you can do today that will help you learn about this new Authentic True Core Value and begin to develop this new Authentic True Core Value?

- What is one action step you are doing with your goal that is working?

- What makes this action step work so well for you?

- What would your goal be like if it was perfect?

- What is missing, which if it were present, would make your goal be perfect?

- What action steps can you take to put in what's missing and have your perfect goal manifest in your life?

- Will you commit to doing that?

- What in the past has gotten in the way or has stopped you from keeping your commitment?

- What do you need to have present or put in place, today, to support you in keeping your commitment?

- In what ways has holding yourself accountable today made you more valuable?

- In what ways has committing to the action steps in the past week made you more valuable?

- How have committing to the action steps and accountability method allowed you to feel more empowered?

The above action and accountability questions are to support you in reaching your goals. You may find that all of the questions or just a few of the questions best support you. Choose those questions that resonate with you, that inspire you and motivate you to hold yourself accountable in reaching your goals. Remember, you can always hire a lifestyle coach or seek out a friend to hold you accountable to as well, until you feel you have developed a positive habit of action and accountability.

Over thinking things never gets you anywhere and takes the fun out of life. Use your heart, intuition, mind, action and accountability. As long as you keep telling yourself that "fine" is enough for you, then fine is all you will keep receiving. If you want to move beyond just "fine" in your life, then action is required. Know you deserve the best and it is your choice.

That vision you've set for yourself, commit to pursuing the specific steps on your Uber Empowerment Lifestyle Plan and you will achieve. You will get there! And remember...YOU rock!

Know That You Have Support

You have a deeper intelligence. More than just using your brain and logic for making choices in your life. You can rely upon your body, mind, heart, and spirit for support and to learn, solve problems, and make sense of the world. You can integrate all of these methods of intelligence: logical approach, emotional, intuitive, details and past lessons and life experiences to shift form trying to predict your world, to using your creativity and authenticity to respond to the world. Practicing this can help you eventually flow more easily with life.

You've read this book, up to this last chapter. For added support, from time to time, you can re-read those areas of the book that most resonated with you and inspired you. Reviewing your Uber Lifestyle Empowerment Plan each day or weekly can be a powerful way to hold yourself accountable for meeting your goals.

Respecting and honoring your self is enough to invest in learning new tools, skills and methods such as the exercises and approaches found in this book. Spending time and energy toward learning more about your unique skills and feeling strong and confident to BE your unique self, can be challenging at times, maybe the most challenging experiences you may have, but will also be the most rewarding. Because once you've found your authentic true core values and have embraced the feeling of empowerment, you can begin to live the life you were meant to live and draw upon this feeling of self-confidence and positive energy when you need additional support. This is listening to your inner guidance and loving your self enough to hold yourself accountable to your inner guidance.

You can rely on the knowledge of contrast in your life and being aware of when you are living with contrast. Contrast tends to show up in your life when you have a high level of desire for something, such as wanting to meet the love of your life, and a high level of resistance or believing it is not possible and feeling discouraged. If you are living with contrast in your life and are unconscious about this, the situation will not change and it could increase feelings of discouragement. Contrast can block you from having what you want in your life, and can keep you from being accountable for your actions.

These limited beliefs we have discussed in chapter 9 and how they are, just beliefs and thoughts, that we keep thinking again and again. These thoughts create feelings in us and those feelings are the vibrations that attract our circumstances to us. By being more aware of the contrast we can choose to focus in on our personal power. Our personal power can help us create a life of happiness, balance, abundance and love.

Contrast can show up in your life such as when you find yourself procrastinating on a project, angry at someone or feeling depressed. You can apply the Ten Elements for the right Mindset to shift to a place of peace or finding a resolution.

Let's take a look at my client, Becky, who was in contrast about finding the love of her life. Becky was Aware that she had limited beliefs about finding the love of her life and if it was really even possible, now that she was 45 years old. Becky also was aware of the thoughts of resistance she would have sometimes, before her date even rang the doorbell. Becky would have thoughts about how bad the night would go and did she really even want to go on another date with this person considering the qualities that bothered her on the last date with this person? These thoughts caused Becky to feel more and more discouraged and depressed about her situation and the evening with her date she was about to head out to.

She Accepted, fully, that she was feeling discouraged and depressed about it. She was Willing to make a shift out of contrast because she no longer wanted to stay single the rest of her life and she was willing to let go of the negative and limited beliefs and feelings she had. Becky created a very strong desire of how her life could be when she met the love of her life and how she wanted to feel having this person in her life.

Becky and I then discussed how she can become more Self-Loving/ Self-Disciplined when the resisting beliefs, thoughts and discouraging emotions would come up. Becky wanted to commit to practice a self-loving action of turning the unlimited belief and thoughts into more positive and empowering thoughts. She chose positive affirmations that resonated with her and caused a positive, loving feeling inside of her. Becky would use these positive affirmations whenever negative thoughts and negative emotions would creep in.

Next, we Arranged for Success by creating an action plan where Becky would keep track each day of the number of times she would catch herself having these dis-empowering feelings and resistant thoughts. Becky was committed to write down her act of self love/self-discipline of positive phrases about meeting the love of her life. We agreed that she would Monitor her Actions by holding herself accountable. At the end of each week, if Becky had less than 10 occurrences of the resistant thoughts and negative emotions, she could give herself an Uber Reward such as buy herself a new item of clothing for the next new date she had.

Eventually, Becky transitioned out of her old ways of thinking and old ways of feeling. She no longer had a high level of resistance to what she so highly desired. Becky was now enjoying feeling more <u>balance</u> and <u>happiness</u> in her life.

Know that every opportunity in life, good or bad, will provide greater clarity about what we truly want. Try not to judge a situation as "good" or "bad" but to be open to what you can learn from the situation. When we choose "good" or "bad" as a way to judge a situation or experience, this is actually choosing to give up our personal power, we are saying we are powerless and looking for confirmation in our life that those limited beliefs, negative thoughts and emotions we had are supporting our sense of powerlessness, helplessness.

Choosing to re-frame a situation and see things you do not want as "contrast" can help you to ask those questions that lead you to discover what it is that is so wanting to be born, what part of yourself needs to be loved and embrace and what old thoughts and beliefs are causing your feelings that attract these situations? Choosing an empowering approach like this will allow you to view your life as a series of wonderful opportunities to allow you the lessons to be learned and your personal power to shine through. Remember you are exactly where you need to be in your personal journey in life, accepting that everything that happens is for a reason and allows us to look for the lesson.

There are other ways to find the support you may need, to help you continue to hold yourself accountable for reaching your goals and living out your Authentic True Core Values, as often as possible. For example, have you ever had such a person in your life who, maybe years have gone by and you finally see them, you pick up right where you left off, you seem to re-connect immediately. This can be a wonderful connection, this person is a dear friend, soul mate, mentor, coach and meant to be there for you.

Often it can help to have a friend to reach out to during challenging times or a mentor or lifestyle coach. An empowering thought to remember: don't fear the unknown, embrace it as a part of yourself and trust that the right people who can encourage you and support you during the times you most need them, will be there at the right time. A good listener seems to actively focus on the information you tell them. You can recognize a good listener because a good listener will often say, "I HEAR what you are FEELING". And you feel understood.

If we were to embrace another in all of their totality and support them in all their dreams, perhaps this is unconditional love. We can forgive, heal and love ourselves and others with the truth of our hearts. True friends fill your heart with joy. A true friend's words and gestures you always FEEL in your heart, no doubts, no guessing. BE a true friend in return. Having true friends who can support you in your life during challenging times and to be there to share celebrations with, makes life more fulfilling.

Showing love to another can be as simple as supporting them in their dreams and goals. When you know your Authentic Life Purpose, just a quick check in with your Inner Guidance, can keep you on YOUR path and you can make your choices in the quickest and simplest way. I really think shared knowledge makes life richer. When you are grateful for someone, you feel it in your heart and these are the best people to surround yourself with for positive support in your life.

Uber Celebrations & Rewards

Remember to celebrate what you DID accomplish so far, even the little steps count. Remember to celebrate along the way... celebrate all your accomplishments no matter how small they may appear to others. They can be your success building motivators.

Filling a whole day with simple pleasures can bring so much fulfillment and abundance. What are some simple pleasures you can enjoy daily?

The reward should relate to your Authentic True Core Values. Is the reward an expression of your personal value? Or is it just an excuse for consumerism? Answering this question will put you in the right direction.

Why are rewards important? According to Nora Valkow, M.D., she states that, "Giving yourself rewards for a behavior engages the dopamine system in your brain and will associate the positive outcome with it, which will help you form the habit." Choosing to reward yourself along the way will help keep you on track and sticking to your positive habits and Authentic True Core Values.

Remember, it can often take two to three weeks of continued practice before a new behavior becomes a habit. Keeping this in mind, you can recall on this short term goal and know that with in three weeks you will have developed a new habit, new behavior, rewarding yourself a long the way. Once you have mastered this new behavior into your life, you may find that the new behavior IS the reward.

We can look at food choices or exercise as examples. Eliminating sugar for 21 days, or two to three weeks, and choosing to eat healthy food choices, the cravings for sugar will go away. You may find you don't need to reward yourself once you've reached your goal and notice the cravings going away. It is similar with exercise, once you have developed the habit of exercising, you may find you crave the positive mental and physiological effects exercise has on your body and this "craving" will automatically have you exercising, which is now your "reward". Until you reach these short term goals of new behaviors, little rewards along the way can help. Rewards such as getting a massage or new workout clothes can keep you motivated and on track.

Celebrating along the way can help you recognize that you DID actually go from "there" to "here" and reflecting on the lessons you may have learned along the way, celebrating how well you overcame obstacles to stay on your path and reach your goal. One of the most important celebrations I tell my clients that they can do for themselves, is to ask themselves the following questions:

- What Authentic True Core Value or Positive Habit have I accomplished that I am proud of?

- What were the lessons I learned along the way?

- What were the roadblocks I overcame?

- In what areas of my life have I grown and how have I grown?

By going through these questions your answers will provide you a way to feel empowered to your accountability, showing you your personal progress and where you can improve, tweak, change – and celebrate all that is working, right now, in your life for having reached these goals. Your answers will provide great insight to you about your Authentic Life Purpose. Taking time to celebrate all you've accomplished and acknowledging your growth along the way, is part of enjoying a fulfilling life. And always remember your sense of humor when your weakness/ shortcomings pop up.

You deserve the best, always, allow the abundance into your life. Happily receive any and all gifts – it is your turn. Believe in the reality of your dreams until you become what you want to be. YOUR dreams, thoughts and efforts will make a big difference in the World.

Appendix

Uber Empowerment Lifestyle Plan
(Example)

Tier One – Feeling & Thinking Your Uber Best

Uber Self-Improvements to help me feel and think my Uber Best:

- Eat less sugar and begin to choose the right foods for energy, balance and optimal health
- Discover fun and creative exercise/workouts that connect my mind, body and soul
- Manage stress to enjoy a balanced, quality life

Nutrition to Feel & Think Your Uber Best

Goals of proper nutrition daily in order to feel and think my Uber best. They are the following:

- Making sure my muscles are adequately fueled
- Prevent dehydration stay hydrated
- Prevent low blood sugar (hypoglycemia)
- Ensuring that my entire body, especially my brain, receives the fuel and nutrients it needs for optimal functioning

A. Foods to Include are Organic, Whole Foods such as:

- Lean protein including turkey chicken, lamb, lean red meat, seafood
- Vegetables and fruit
- Nuts, eggs and egg whites
- Protein powders: egg white, rice, whey

B. Beverages:

- Green Tea
- Organic Regular Coffee (no more than two cups per day)
- High alkaline water
- Wine (in moderation, one to three glasses per week)

C. Nutritional Supplements:

- High Quality Multivitamin daily
- Pro-biotic daily
- CoQ10 60 - 100mg daily
- EPA-DHA daily
- Magnesium 200mg - 400mg each evening

D. Soul Nourishment:

- Read inspirational book each morning, upon awakening
- Read inspirational quotes through out the day
- Spend time in nature each day
- Listen to uplifting music that soothes the soul and makes the spirit soar

Uber Energetic Movement® to Feel & Think Your Uber Best
Uber Energetic Movement® Schedule

Week One

MONDAY	Run hills followed by 20 minute stretching session
TUESDAY	Body Sculpting, Back/Chest/Abs
WEDNESDAY	Interval Training, 20 minute Stair Machine & 20 minute Stationary Bike
THURSDAY	Power walk on the beach
FRIDAY	Body Sculpting, Legs
SATURDAY	Run, flat terrain
SUNDAY	Yoga (Hatha)

Week Two

MONDAY	Body Sculpting – Shoulders/Triceps/Biceps
TUESDAY	Run–on beach/sand
WEDNESDAY	Ashtanga Yoga
THURSDAY	Roller skate or roller blade or dance or Pilates
FRIDAY	Rest
SATURDAY	Circuit training – strength training mixed with bursts of cardiovascular exercises
SUNDAY	Hiking with a group or a friend

Week Three

MONDAY	Yoga Vinyasa
TUESDAY	Body Sculpting/Strength Training – Back/Chest/Abs
WEDNESDAY	Run and workout abs
THURSDAY	Body Sculpting/Strength Training – Legs
FRIDAY	Rest
SATURDAY	Interval cardiovascular exercising treadmill 20 minutes and stationary bike
SUNDAY	Roller blade or roller skate or ride your bike (grab a friend!)

Week Four

MONDAY	Boot Camp Class in your community or at your gym –try something new!
TUESDAY	Rest
WEDNESDAY	Run with a friend or group in your community, if possible or find a track in your area to mix up the different terrain
THURSDAY	Yoga Kundalini or Pilates or Dance (yes, even going out in the evening and dancing with friends counts towards creative movement!).
FRIDAY	Body Sculpting/Strength Training: Shoulders/Triceps/Biceps and Abs
SATURDAY	Saturday: Walking – find some hills and grab a friend
SUNDAY	Run/Walk intervals outside in park or at the beach

Balance & Stress Management Strategies
to Feel & Think Your Uber Best

A. Daily

- Read Inspirational Books/Quotes/Articles 10–20 minutes in the morning and again in the evening, read inspirational quotes through out the day.

- Meditate

- Writing for Awareness journal, write inspirational articles, quotes, e–mails.

- Review Authentic Life Purpose Statement

- Include a form of Uber Energetic Movement

B. Weekly

- Music as therapy

- Time in Nature

- Quality Conversations with friends/family

C. Monthly

- Massage

- Review Authentic Goals

- Review Uber Empowerment Lifestyle Plan

D. Annually

- Trip/Vacation to visit sister

- Trip/Vacation spend Christmas with Family

- Visit a new place, destination−country, city −consider options: fly, drive, cruise

- Learn something new − take a course of interest, try a new activity

Tier Two – Recognizing Your Uber Authentic Self Leads To True Fulfillment Living Your Optimal Life

A. List the Energy Zappers in your life.

Consider all areas of your life. Choose the best method for how you will manage each one of your Energy Zappers. Remember, you may have some areas in your life where there are NO Energy Zappers and others where there are many Energy Zappers. This is okay. Get the Energy Zappers down on paper for you to see and choose the best method for you to manage each one of your listed Energy Zappers:

Work/Career/Professional Life:

- E-mail overload/overwhelmed.
  Solution:
  e-mails – answer in the morning and again late
  afternoon (keep personal e-mails separate from work
  e-mails, as one option OR choose to only answer
  work e-mails in the morning and late afternoon.
  Personal e-mails once daily.

- Messy desk with post it notes.
  Solution:
  No more sticky/post it notes. Write on daily
  planner only: tasks needed to be completed
  that day, appointments.

- Volunteering too often my expertise to others business,
  feeling unfulfilled when I have not focused enough on
  my projects that promote my business.

Solution:
Know it is okay to say "no" to that last request.

Relationships:

- Phone calls not returned to family/friends, allowing too many days to go by.

  Solution:
  Returning all phone calls within a 24 hour
  time frame

- Desire quality friendships and quality relationships with family, significant other.

  Solution:
  Develop quality relationships by really listening, giving full attention in all interactions.

- Not planning ahead to see friends/hard to match up last minute "get together".

  Solution:
  Call and actually set a date, even if a few weeks ahead, commit to the event/time.

Community:

- Wanting to make time for giving in community with out feeling drained.

  Solution:
  Make time for Community Reiki Circle once a month.

- Solicitors outside of stores asking for signature to causes can be annoying.

  Solution:
  Know it is okay to say "no", realize it is all on how you say "no". Be firm but give a warm smile and say "no thank you".

Finances:

- Review usage of minutes on cell phone plan, not using full minutes?

  Solution:
  Change plan on Thursday/March 18 @ 4:00 p.m.

- How important is Cable T.V? Not watching/utilizing ALL of the Cable Plan?

  Solution:
  Change Cable Plan/downgrade on Thursday/March 18 @ 4:30 p.m.

- Manage bills.

  Solution:
  Pay Bills once a month: First of each Month, pay bills. Review usage of all services such as cable, cell phone plan and any subscriptions – not using them to the full advantage, delete these or change/downgrade the plan on Thursday/March 18 @ 4:45 p.m.

Home Environment:

- Messy stuff laying around becomes a distraction from work.

  Solution:
  Straighten up/put things away after using them – Daily.

- Drainer – items in garage not using.

  Solution:
  Clean out garage: March 20 @ 3:00 p.m. Allow one hour and donate items to charity.

- Car has defective part, still covered under warranty. Know this needs to be fixed, get it off my mind.

  Solution:
  Make Appointment to get defective belt/tensioner repaired on car, March 18th.

Emotional:

- Keep energy balanced through out the day.

  Solution:
  Take short breaks, brisk walk, meditate for 20 minutes, stretch for 10 minutes, call a friend.

Health/Wellness:

- Need to make appointment for dentist cleaning/check up.

Solution:
Call and make an appointment for Monday March 29th for the afternoon.

- Would like to take better care of health/wellness through preventative treatments.

    Solution:
    Make appointments for acupuncture for overall well being. Call and schedule appointments on Monday, May 24.

Spirituality:

- Not feeling inner connected, seeking higher awareness.

    Solution:
    Read one new inspirational book per month, meditate daily.

B. Uber Empowerment Rituals & Rewards (be sure to mark each Uber Empowerment Rituals & Rewards on your calendar):

- *A walk on the beach, in the sunshine Monday @ 1:00 p.m. And on Wednesday at 2:00 p.m.*

- *Spend time with friends: Wednesday/March 17 @ 6:30 p.m. and Saturday/March 20 @ 4:00 p.m.*

- *Meditate: daily for 30 minutes between 2:00 p.m. ~ 4:30 p.m.*

- *Movie March 29 @ 5:00 p.m.*

- *Visit Museum on Thursday @ 3:00 p.m.*

C. Release Negative Experiences to Create Peace.

List all of your past and recent experiences that hold negative emotions and thoughts. List an action step, perhaps a specific date you will schedule to reflect on what the lesson was to be learned and release any lingering negative emotions and thoughts.

Experience 1

Job lay off or not receiving the desired Promotion.

Action Date to Reflect

March 16, 2010

Lingering Feelings/Thoughts

Fear, wronged, self-doubt, sad, confused, anxious, anger

Lessons Learned

Thankful for the wonderful educational knowledge, the strong professional relationships built with clients, opportunity to focus on greatest strengths and natural gifts and to begin a career that allows, true authentic self to shimmer!

Experience 2

Divorce or Break-up

Action Date to Reflect

April 12, 2010

Lingering Feelings/Thoughts

Hurt, confused, wronged, sad, angry

Lessons Learned

Grateful for what you were able to learn about yourself by choosing to be in the relationship with this person. Thankful for Clarity, showing you the right information you need to enlighten you with what you really value in life and in relationships.

D. Five Authentic Rules to live life by and what steps to begin to integrate these rules into daily life.

1. Live a Healthy Lifestyle

Integrate this rule into my life:

Follow nutrition plan, creative movement plan and manage stress to feel my best and think my best in order to recognize my true Uber Authentic Self and to be my best Uber Authentic Self.

2. Live my life with Mindfulness

Integrate this rule into my life:

Allow myself plenty of time, don't over schedule, don't rush, focus on each moment and listen to others with 100% full attention.

3. Feel Empowered in the Choices I make.

Integrate this rule into my life:

Make choices I feel in alignment with and encourage others to do so as well. Choose choices in life that are meaningful to me, where I want to give my best efforts, choices I feel good.

4. Live with an Open Mind and Non-judgment

Integrate this rule into my life:

Notice the strengths and positive in everyone and in myself.

5. Abide by the Golden Rule.

Integrate this rule into my life:

Think before speaking

Lend a hand

Offer a kind word

Just listen

Notice others strengths and give them compliments

Compassion toward others

Discovering Your Uber Authentic Self

A. Uber Authentic Life Purpose Statement:

Example One:

> *"My Uber Authentic Life Purpose work is to be supportive of self and others, by living a healthy and balanced lifestyle through nourishing mind, body and soul; contributing through work that offers authenticity and fulfillment, sharing quality time and connecting through quality conversations, making the world a better place."*

Example Two:

> *"My Uber Authentic Life Purpose is to embrace knowledge and share inspirational wisdom with the world through learning, writing and empowering myself and others."*

B. Authentic True Core Values

- *Live a Healthy Lifestyle*
- *Communicating through Quality Conversations*
- *Writing/Creating to Inspire Others*
- *Love*
- *Spirituality/Wisdom and Reading*

Prioritizing Your Authentic Values

A. Creating Goals that allow you to live your Authentic Values: Write your goals down below along with completion dates for each goal.

Short-term Goals

60 Day Goals:

Complete Writing Project – 4/30/2010 completion date

Grow business by adding new clients, 5/15/10 completion date

Re-model project – 5/31/2010 completion date

90 Day Goals:

Grow business by building account base/new clients per month by 6/1/2010

Complete 2 Continuing Education Certifications 7/31/2010

Complete Home-Improvement Projects – 5/31/2010

Long-term Goals

Two Year Goals:

Conduct monthly workshops/seminars

Maintain account base and grow new business each month

Continuing Education Certification Classes

Vacation to somewhere new

Five Year Goals:

Open new office location in local community

Write book series and articles

Vacation to somewhere new

B. Adding New Authentic Values

1. Discovery: my definition of this new value is to add more authentic pursuits, visit new places, try a new restaurant, shop at a new boutique

2. Joining Others: my definition of this new value is to socialize with new groups to meet new people who share like minded interests

Tier Three: Become Empowered To BE Your Uber Empowered Self

Your Success & Embracing Change

A. Your Language of Success. Describe your definition of success:

Success is feeling fulfilled in your personal and professional life, knowing you are using your natural gifts and greatest strengths to do and be the best you can be.

B. What needs to change in your life for you to succeed? List all the things that will need to change in your life for you to succeed with your goals.

* *Dating/Marriage: Alone time – creating a balance of alone time and couple time.*
* *Growing Business: More structured schedule.*
* *Continued Education: Dedicate extra time towards the workshop/class (less social time, for a time period).*
* *Conducting Workshops/Seminars: some travel required.*

C. List some past situations in your life where you experienced Trusting the Choice you made and any feelings you had, messages you received, words of affirmation you heard that you were on the right path, anything along the way that was associated with that Self-Trust:

- Coming across a company, by coincident, while researching for a writing project and experiencing a "knowing" that resonating with the company, even though they were not hiring at the time.
- Selecting the right person for your team to create a successful business project. Knowing this connection was something higher than just the two of you.
- Choosing to leave a relationship for the highest good of both people involved.

Letting go of limited beliefs

A. Write down the limited beliefs you hold and next to that limited belief, create your new, positive belief:

Old Limited Belief	New Positive Belief
I will never get this assignment done in time.	I am confident that I will manage my time wisely and complete this assignment.
I can't believe I did that, I am so dumb!	What can I learn from this experience?
I seem to keep meeting jerks, I really dread dating.	It is fun to meet new people through dating and learn what their best qualities are.
I can't afford that.	I manage my money wisely.
I wouldn't succeed at something like that!	These are all the reasons I can give this a try and why I would succeed at this.

Plan to live your Uber Empowerment Lifestyle - Accountability is Empowering

A. List the areas in your life where you would like to <u>Act Courageously</u>. Then, list Action Steps on how you will Act Courageously (holding yourself Accountable):

Area to Act Courageously: Grow Business

Action Steps:

- Daily review of Authentic Life Purpose Statement and Authentic True Core Values.
- Weekly Review of Goals my progress, add a new goal, changes that need to be embraced and dealt with.

Area to Act Courageously: Spend Quality Time with Family

Action Steps:

- Attend more outings together.
- Give full attention during conversations, practice being a good listener.

B. List the various ways you plan to receive support for living your Uber Empowerment Plan (encouragement from family; friends; a support group; hire a lifestyle coach; talk to a mentor):

- *Coaching*
- *Family*
- *Friends*
- *Attend seminars*

Write down the Uber Celebrations & Rewards you will give yourself when you've reached a goal. Complete this for your short term goals, long term goals. You can also create a reward or celebrate when you've added a new Authentic True Core Value into your life and you've seen progress over a period of one to three weeks in how you've lived this new Authentic True Core Value.

C. Celebration & Uber Rewards

Celebrating/Uber Rewards for reaching 60 Day Goals/90 Day Goals:

- *Massage/Spa Day Reward for completing my book.*
- *Special bottle of Wine for growing business through increasing account base.*
- *Celebrate with a nice dinner out upon completion of Continuing Education Certification.*

Celebrating/Uber Rewards for reaching Yearly Goals:

1. Successful workshops/seminar – take a trip to a destination to relax, celebrate and rejuvenate.

2. Opening new office location – hold an Opening Night Event to celebrate grand opening.

Celebrating Ideas and/or Uber Rewards for living New Authentic True Core Values:

1. Buy a memorable small gift from one of the new places visited.

2. Buy new outfit to wear for the next night out in Joining Others

Uber Empowerment Lifestyle Plan
(My Plan)

Tier One – Feeling & Thinking Your Uber Best

Uber Self-Improvements to help me feel and think my Uber Best:

Nutrition to Feel & Think Your Uber Best

Goals of proper nutrition daily in order to feel and think my Uber best. They are the following:

    A. Foods to Include are Organic, Whole Foods such as:

_____

_____

_____

_____

    B. Beverages:

_____

_____

_____

_____

C. Nutritional Supplements:

_____

_____

_____

D. Nourishment for the Soul:

_____

_____

_____

Uber Energetic Movement® to Feel & Think Your Uber Best
Uber Energetic Movement® Schedule

Week One

MONDAY	
TUESDAY	
WEDNESDAY	
THURSDAY	
FRIDAY	
SATURDAY	
SUNDAY	

Week Two

MONDAY	
TUESDAY	
WEDNESDAY	
THURSDAY	
FRIDAY	
SATURDAY	
SUNDAY	

Week Three

MONDAY	
TUESDAY	
WEDNESDAY	
THURSDAY	
FRIDAY	
SATURDAY	
SUNDAY	

Week Four

MONDAY	
TUESDAY	
WEDNESDAY	
THURSDAY	
FRIDAY	
SATURDAY	
SUNDAY	

Balance & Stress Management Strategies to Feel & Think Your Uber Best

A. Daily

1. _____

2. _____

3. _____

_____

B. Weekly

1. _____

2. _____

3. _____

_____

C. Monthly

1. _____

2. _____

3. _____

_____

D. Annually

1. _____

2. _____

3. _____

_____

Tier Two – Recognizing Your Uber Authentic Self Leads To True Fulfillment Living Your Optimal Life

A. List the Energy Zappers in your life.

Consider all areas of your life. Choose the best method for how you will manage each one of your Energy Zappers. Remember, you may have some areas in your life where there are NO Energy Zappers and others where there are many Energy Zappers. This is okay. Get the Energy Zappers down on paper for you to see and choose the best method for you to manage each one of your listed Energy Zappers:

Work/Career/Professional Life:

1. _____

2. _____

3. _____

_____

Relationships:

1. _____

2. _____

3. _____

_____

Community:

1. _____

2. _____

3. _____

_____

Finances:

1. _____

2. _____

3. _____

_____

Home Environment:

1. _____

2. _____

3. _____

_____

Emotional:

1. _____

2. _____

3. _____

_____

Health/Wellness:

1. _____

2. _____

3. _____

_____

Spirituality:

1. _____

2. _____

3. _____

_____

B. Uber Empowerment Rituals & Rewards: (be sure to mark each Uber Empowerment Ritual & Reward on your calendar):

1. _____

2. _____

3. _____

_____

_____

_____

_____

_____

_____

_____

_____

_____

C. Release Negative Experiences to Create Peace.

List all of your past and recent experiences that hold negative emotions and thoughts. List an action step, perhaps a specific date you will schedule to reflect on what the lesson was to be learned and release any lingering negative emotions and thoughts.

Experience

_____

_____

_____

Action Date to Reflect

_____

Lingering Feelings/Thoughts

_____

_____

_____

Lessons Learned

_____

_____

_____

_____

D. Five Authentic Rules to live life by and what steps to begin to integrate these rules into daily life.

1. Live a Healthy Lifestyle

Integrate this rule into my life:

_____

_____

_____

2. Live my life with Mindfulness

Integrate this rule into my life:

_____

_____

_____

3. Feel Empowered in the Choices I make

Integrate this rule into my life:

_____

_____

_____

4. Live with an Open Mind and Non-judgment

Integrate this rule into my life:

_____

_____

_____

_____

_____

_____

5. Abide by the Golden Rule

Integrate this rule into my life:

_____

_____

_____

_____

_____

_____

Discovering Your Uber Authentic Self

A. Uber Authentic Life Purpose Statement:

Example One:

_____

_____

_____

_____

_____

Example Two:

_____

_____

_____

_____

_____

B. Authentic True Core Values

_____

_____

_____

_____

_____

Prioritizing Your Authentic Values

A. Creating Goals that allow you to live your Authentic Values: Write your goals down below along with completion dates for each goal.

Short-term Goals

60 Day Goals:

_____

_____

_____

_____

90 Day Goals:

_____

_____

_____

_____

Long-term Goals

Two Year Goals:

_____

_____

_____

_____

1

0**APPENDIX**

Five Year Goals:

_____

_____

_____

_____

B. Adding New Authentic Values

_____

_____

_____

_____

_____

_____

_____

_____

_____

_____

_____

_____

_____

_____

_____

_____

_____

269

Tier Three: Become Empowered To BE
Your Uber Empowered Self

<u>Your Success & Embracing Change</u>

A. Your Language of Success. Describe your definition of success:

_____

_____

_____

_____

_____

B. What needs to change in your life for you to succeed? List all the things that will need to change in your life for you to succeed with your goals.

_____

_____

_____

_____

_____

_____

_____

_____

_____

_____

C. List some past situations in your life where you experienced Trusting the Choice you made and any feelings you had, messages you received, words of affirmation you heard that you were on the right path, anything along the way that was associated with that Self-Trust:

_____

_____

_____

_____

_____

_____

_____

Letting Go Of Limited Beliefs

A. Write down the limited beliefs you hold and next to that limited belief, create your new, positive belief:

Old Limited Belief	New Positive Belief

Plan to live your Uber Empowerment Lifestyle - Accountability is Empowering

A. List the areas in your life where you would like to <u>Act Courageously</u>. Then, list Action Steps on how you will Act Courageously (holding yourself Accountable):

_____

_____

_____

_____

_____

B. List the various ways you plan to receive support for living your Uber Empowerment Plan (encouragement from family; friends; a support group; hire a lifestyle coach; talk to a mentor):

_____

_____

_____

_____

Write down the Uber Celebrations & Rewards you will give yourself when you've reached a goal. Complete this for your short term goals, long term goals. You can also create a reward or celebrate when you've added a new Authentic True Core Value into your life and you've seen progress over a period of one to three weeks in how you've lived this new Authentic True Core Value.

Celebrating/Uber Rewards for reaching <u>30 Day Goals</u>:

_____

_____

_____

_____

Celebrating/Uber Rewards for reaching <u>60 Day Goals</u>:

_____

_____

_____

_____

Celebrating/Uber Rewards for reach <u>90 Day Goals</u>:

_____

_____

_____

_____

Celebrating/Uber Rewards for reaching <u>Yearly Goals</u>:

_____

_____

_____

_____

Celebrating/Uber Rewards for living new Authentic True Core Values:

_____

_____

_____

_____

Dear Reader

*"Faith that the thing can be
done is essential to any great achievement".
- Thomas N. Carruther*

You now have the tools I have provided, to create your own Uber Empowerment Lifestyle Plan, at your own pace, that will allow you to achieve your own Uber Self. Focus on your inner awareness, stay connected to your inner-self and your Authentic True Core Values – your natural gifts to offer to the world. Know that you can call on your Uber Empowered Being and carry it with you each day, every hour, every second, every heartbeat at a time and you'll feel that intuitive nudge, that subtle yet distinct vibe that tells you, you are being True to yourself and allowing yourself to BE your Uber Self.

Every lifestyle choice we make to be sedentary or to exercise, from what we put into our mouths, to how we choose to live our Authentic True Core Values, make up our Whole Self—body, mind and spirit – now as well as who we will become in the future.

"Seek out that particular mental attribute
which makes you feel most deeply and vitally alive, along with which
comes the inner voice which says, "This is the real me,"
and when you have found that attitude, follow It".
- William James

Attract clarity through *your* Truth and manifest what you want to create in *your* life. Feel inspired and empowered to find your true, powerful inner spirit and acquire the flexibility and balance to live each day with whatever life might throw your way. Remember to be grateful. Being grateful allows more inspiration and wisdom into your soul and more abundance into your life.

You may have discovered only one tool out of my book for you to integrate into your lifestyle or you may have found the entire book had tools for you to use. Keep in mind, it may be a few years or in a few months, you find that you want to change some of your Uber Empowerment Lifestyle plan – perfect! Change is good. Revisit these tools when you need to.

If the methods in this book resonated with you, and you would like more inspiration, guidance and accountability, you are invited to continue your personal growth and professional development through coaching sessions with me. You can visit my website for further information on the various coaching packages at www.uberempowerment.com.

Feel free to contact me and tell me about your Uber Empowerment Lifestyle Plan. I always enjoy hearing a new powerful and inspirational quote, so feel free to share that with me, as well. All my best to you and I wish you Uber Empowerment, success and fulfillment in all areas of your life.

About The Author

Nancy is a Holistic Lifestyle Empowerment Coach. She helps inspire those who are ready to recognize and maximize their true strengths and to become their optimal self. Empowering clients through looking at the whole person, holistically – mind, body and soul to feel and be their Uber Self. Uber is defined as the ultimate, the best, top, literal meaning "above" in German. Nancy believes one must feel their best in order to think their best and be their best in life. Through her Holistic Lifestyle Empowerment Coaching she will help you feel your best and provide the right Mindset Approach to ensure you are living your true core values in life every day or as often as possible. She looks at each client as an individual. Nancy can assist you in creating your own empowerment plan that will guide you to trust your powerful inner spirit to choose the lifestyle choices that will align you with living a life that you really want and love. As your personal coach she will work with you to realize what you want personally and professionally and support you along the way.

Nancy completed her B.A. in communication at Arizona State University with an emphasis in Interpersonal Communication. She has a Therapeutic Lifestyle Educator Certificate and has completed Level One in Reiki Energy work. She is also a Certified Professional Coach. In addition, her professional background consists of nutritional consulting and sales and business resource networking.

Her personal and professional experiences have led Nancy to want to inspire and help others. Her ambition to reach her Uber Self level in life and still enjoy a balanced lifestyle has led her to research, learn and experiment the best plan that would help her achieve this. She has chosen a path that allows her to live with mind/heart connection and empowerment. Through one on one coaching sessions with clients, she feels so blessed to know she has a part in improving their lives and helping them to feel empowered to become their optimal, Uber self. She truly loves to help and inspire others to become their full potential!

Some interests and activities that Nancy enjoys are walking, running, the beach, strength training. She has won five medals in various 10k races. She enjoys good wine, sunsets, quality time with friends and family, sharing good conversations, reading and writing. She especially enjoys e-mails from readers who have enjoyed her articles and her quotes and interactions on Facebook, LinkedIn and Twitter.

Please enjoy your visit at her website: www.uberempowerment.com.